From sacred seed …

to sharing bread …

...The One Loaf

an everyday celebration

Joy Mead

WILD GOOSE PUBLICATIONS

The publishers gratefully acknowledge the assistance of a grant from the
Drummond Trust in producing this book

Distributed in Australia by
Willow Connection Pty Ltd,
Unit 4A, 3-9 Kenneth Road, Manly Vale, NSW 2093, Australia

and in New Zealand by
Pleroma Christian Supplies,
Higginson St., Otane 4170, Central Hawkes Bay, New Zealand

Permission to reproduce any part of this work in Australia
or New Zealand should be sought from Willow Connection.

Printed in China

Contents

Contributors

Foreword

In my last pastorate before I retired, there was a man in the congregation whom I remember more clearly than many of the other church members, and not for obvious reasons – he wasn't a prominent office-bearer or elder, nor did he play the organ or serve on any committees. He was in every sense 'just' an ordinary member of our church.

He was short and strongly built, gentle and almost taciturn, with a good face and trust-inspiring hands. He had been a baker all his life, rising daily at three o'clock in the morning to walk down to the bakery in the town centre where he worked.

It was he who throughout the years baked the communion bread for the congregation – small, flat, round loaves, doughy and golden; you could smell them as soon as you entered church on communion Sundays.

For the sharing of bread and wine the worshippers would come in relays and stand in a semicircle around the communion table. Each time I broke off a piece of bread and pressed it into the people's waiting hands, they would (being liturgically literate!) respond to the words 'The body of Christ, given for you' by saying 'Amen'. Not so the baker! He would look me intently in the eye and quietly say, 'Thank you.' If we had been a Greek-speaking congregation, he would have said, 'Eucharisto.'

I must admit that to remember those eye-to-eye encounters still moves me profoundly: here was a man whose very being and life symbol-ised that whole world-spanning process of grain being sown, harvested, milled, baked and laid on our altars and kitchen tables. His 'thank you' somehow used to give a wider and deeper dimension to what we were doing inside a church building whose opaque and none too clean mock-gothic windows were so high up on the walls that we could not look out through them to see what was going on in the earth-world around us, from which we had come and to which we were bound to return.

Joy Mead's highly original book fascinates me as much as the memory of that baker stays with me. *The One Loaf* is earthy and gutsy, passionate and intuitive, and thus it is far removed from the often tortuous, precious and sometimes pedantic theological tomes – hundreds of them – written to define the meaning and 'explain' the mystery of what is so frequently bandied about as 'the sacrament of unity'. Anyone who has ever attended international and ecumenical assemblies will be able to recall the searing pain of *not* being able to break and share bread together, because the differing hierarchical, theological rulebooks decree that we shouldn't. But in order not to rock the boat named 'Oikumene', there generally has been acquiescence rather than rebellion: 'Yes sir, no sir, three bags full, sir' … *Toujours la politesse.*

Joy and the baker each remind me of an American theologian whom I was privileged to meet at a couple of non-theological, after-hours, post-assembly gatherings in the USA. In one of his most exciting books, Art Cochrane rocks that boat:

> … *the so-called Sacrament of the Lord's Supper, as it is observed in most churches, has little relevance for modern people, precisely because it has little or no relation to eating and drinking outside church walls.*
>
> *With the problems of poverty and hunger, and of the production, distribution and consumption of food, which oppress all people in their daily lives, it has virtually nothing to do; the Lord's Supper has no relation to people's work, their economics and their politics.*
>
> *I came to see that Christendom has tended to drive a wedge – a wedge that is foreign to the Bible – between the sacred and the secular, the soul and the body, the spiritual and the temporal, and thus to drive a wedge between a holy and profane eating and drinking.*[1]

If only Joy and the baker and Art could have met …

So … whenever your loved one puts the toastrack in front of you at the breakfast table, or the baker sells you your hot bread rolls at the village 'fournos' on Mykonos, or your minister breaks the bread in front of your very eyes, think of how you want to respond, with a 'thank-you', an 'eucharisto' or even an 'Amen'. And take Joy's book on thank-you theology with you, to celebrate the day's ordinariness.

Fred Kaan

1 From: *Eating and Drinking with Jesus, An Ethical and Biblical Inquiry,* by Arthur C. Cochrane. Westminster John Knox Press, Louisville, Kentucky, USA, 1974. Used by permission.

Introduction

Beginnings ...

The idea for this book came out of a *Bread of Life* day organised by Kath and Ray Short for the Southampton Methodist District. Speakers that day were Nigel Collinson (then President of the Methodist Conference, now Secretary of the Methodist Conference) who tells a story on page 151, and Jan Sutch Pickard (then Vice President of the Methodist Conference, now Deputy Warden at Iona Abbey and the MacLeod Centre, on Iona) who has made a big contribution to this book.

The Southampton event included workshops with the titles: *Our Daily Bread, The Common Good, Wholeness is Health, The Bread is Rising!, Ways of Seeing, Making Music, Talk Over Bread.* This was more than a talk day. It was a whole-life activity: the *Talk Over Bread* group made the bread which we used for the agape in the afternoon.

My thinking about and over bread (I make all my own) continued and I have been encouraged by thoughts others have shared with me. Everyone seems to enjoy talking about bread – as well as eating it. I'm grateful for the enthusiasm of the other contributors to this book. All of them have given more than their writing. I'm also grateful for the encouragement of Ian and all my family and friends. In particular my good friend Jan Sutch Pickard has always generously supported, encouraged and inspired me. Over the years, Jan and I have shared bread in every way and for that I'm thankful.

My thinking has been particularly about the kitchen as a field of nurturing (making the connection between women at the altar and women at the kitchen table) and the way we experience bread in all its moments: growing, making, breaking, sharing. In bread we see the true connectedness of all life – the uniting of body and soul, spirit and material. Bread is central: right there in the middle of the Lord's Prayer: *Give us this day our daily bread;* central to the eucharist – the sharing. Bread is not just a symbol of life, it is life itself. Without food life is impossible; so eating becomes sacred. Take and eat means take and live. To share food is to share your life. Jesus' disciples accepted bread from him. He, in a simple act, made eating and sharing sacred.

I began to realise that every creative aspect of our living could be included in some way under the title Bread. The problem would not be what to put in but what to leave out!

So this book is about all the stages from sacred seed to beautiful bread, the sowing to the sharing: growing, making, breaking, sharing. We explore the making and the mystery in poetry and prayer, story and recipe. We see how closely interwoven are spiritual and material – how impossible to separate. We learn to love the dailiness of bread (see Jan Sutch Pickard, p.80): the holiness of eating and the justice of sharing. If you feel uncomfortable with some of this heavenly earthiness, just stop and think: are you perhaps one of those 'over-versed in liturgical rubrics'?[1]

Many of the pieces in this book are beginnings. I hope you will allow them to work like yeast in individual lives and communities – so that the whole may be transformed and the words become your words.

Joy Mead,
Great Missenden
Bucks
2000

1 From Joan Puls, *Every Bush is Burning* (WCC, Geneva, 1987, p.7)

The One Loaf

Out of fire it comes
with bodily contours
satisfying to all senses:
a warm loaf; seedy and grainy
soft and being-shaped,
its yeasty smell, homely
and heavenly,
of fungus and damp autumn
woodlands … and the sun's warmth.

All life is here:
ordinary, good and beautiful:
growing things and cow dung,
woody roots and seeds,
bodies of creatures
long dead in the soil;
all in this given
bread of our beginnings;
all in our breaking
and sharing
our one loaf.

Joy Mead

Part One

Harvest Dance

'The corn was orient and immortal wheat, which never should be reaped, nor was ever sown'[1] – and so it was for the 17th-century poet Thomas Traherne. He never lost his childhood sense of eternity and the sheer wonder of being alive – daily, dancing, ordinary wonder. Traherne tells us we'll never enjoy the world aright until we wake 'every morning in heaven …', until we 'see how a grain of sand exhibiteth the wisdom and power of God'. Really seeing things, giving our loving attention to the littleness of a grain of wheat or the stories ordinary people tell, helps us to grow more just and compassionate; gives us greater awareness of what it is we have in our keeping: this everyday, earthy miracle of life. These verses from Brian Wren's hymn put it beautifully:

> The precious seed of life is in our keeping,
> yet if we plant it, and fulfil our trust,
> tomorrow's sun will rise of joy and weeping,
> and shine upon the unjust and the just.
>
> Our calling is to live our human story
> of good and bad, achievement, love and loss,
>   then hand it on to future shame or glory
>   lit by our hope, and leavened by the cross.[2]

So over the next few pages we have beginnings: seeds to save and share. Remember that story of a handful of wheat, five thousand years old, found in the tomb of one of the kings of ancient Egypt. Someone planted the grains and, to the amazement of all, the grains came to life. Then there are today's grains ready for milling. Milling and mills are part of the story, part of our cultural landscape, using the gifts of water and wind to gently mill the sunlight and sweetness out of the grain so that it becomes part of us.

It is sacred, this rhythm: life given, sustained and handed on; saving, sharing, planting, sowing, then reaping – the joy of the harvest and dancing into the sun again. Out of the earthy silence and the dark comes energy – the dance of life. Roman Christians could not wipe out the Celtic festival of Lughnasa that celebrates Lugh, the dancing god of the harvest. The rich, bountiful harvest to be celebrated is the dance of life and so became part (often unrecognised!) of Christian harvest dances, festivals, suppers and services.

So use these poems, stories, prayers … to think about beginnings and harvests – the cycle of life … about the crazy hope, like Martha's (see p.141), that life will burst forth again … and dance.

1 Thomas Traherne, *Centuries* (Mowbray, London and Oxford, 1960, p.14)
2 Brian Wren from 'Come, cradle all the future generations' in *Piece Together Praise*, © 1983 Hope Publishing Company for the USA, Canada, Australia and New Zealand and Stainer and Bell Ltd for all other territories.

Because of the Seed

Once in Baghdad there was a very good sultan, much loved and admired by all his subjects. He was kind and helpful, always energetic and caring, and above all he was just.

Parents are at their best when they are both caring and just, and both kind and strong, and so are teachers and bosses and rulers of all kinds, and in all places and at all times.

How had it come about that the sultan in Baghdad was so wise? What was his secret? Had he been born like this? Was it the way he had been brought up?

The people wondered and asked each other. One day a very wise old storyteller came to Baghdad, and the people asked her opinion. Had the sultan been born caring and just, and kind and strong, or was it the way he had been brought up? Or was it just luck?

'I don't know,' replied the wise old storyteller, 'but I will tell you this. I was here in Baghdad when he was born, and I was invited to the banquet which his father gave to celebrate his birth. All the nobles of Baghdad were there, and they brought a great mass of very expensive presents, in particular piles and heaps of jewels and rare coins.

'I was poor then as I am also poor now, and I could not give the baby any jewels. But what I did was to give him stories. All through his child-hood and teenage years I used to visit him at his parents' mansions, and tell him stories.'

'What were your stories about?' asked the people.

'They were stories about people on journeys, and about people asking questions and searching for answers. When people in my stories are brave, and go on and on journeying and searching, the most wonder-ful things happen to them. Sometimes …'

'Yes?' asked the people. 'Sometimes?'

Sometimes in my stories it's as if people come close to God. Not that I ever use the word God, I dare not name him, I dare not think as big as that.'

'Are you telling the truth?' asked the people. 'Or is this just another of your stories?'

The storyteller smiled, but did not answer.

On the monument which his people made when the good sultan died, there were these few simple words, very carefully and very beautifully crafted:

It was because of the seed sown by the tales.

Wheat Grain

The given beauty of it –
inert in my palm
tender, fragile thing
quietly holding
good for all people,
complex and intricate,
storing life and the means
of life.

The silent wonder of it –
Jack in the beanstalk story:
always ready to sprout
while the sower is away;
fairy story; or miracle:
seed, soil, labour, love;
life, death, rebirth,
Earth's best gift,
seed of freedom
for all our tomorrows.

Joy Mead

The Disciples

(Luke 6:1–5)

We are the disciples –
when we were boys
we scrumped apples,
ate them and threw away the cores.
Now we walk through the fields,
plucking ears of corn,
rubbing them between our palms
and eating the milky, floury kernels.

'Stop that!' shouted the Pharisees.
'Don't you know it's the Sabbath –
how dare you
reap the corn and winnow it?
Next thing we know
you'll be baking it
and setting up shop.
Keep the Sabbath holy!'

Jesus said, 'But they're hungry.
Remember what the Bible says
about great King David:
when his men were starving
he took bread
from the house of God –
the bread offered to God,
the bread that only priests could eat –
and he shared it out
among ordinary people in their need.
What makes the Sabbath holy
is that we do good things on it.

What makes bread blessed
is the sharing.'

We listen to the argument –
all ears, licking our lips –
still savouring the grains of wheat,
free for all,
which were bread in the making,
daily bread
given to us, and God.

Jan Sutch Pickard

Wheat is Life

Give us seedcorn to keep us alive or we shall die
and our land will become a desert.   (Genesis 47:19)

Wheat is life,
we know it
crossing a field
picking the grain heads
rubbing the special sweetness
into our palms:
life in our hands –
tasting, tasting, fullness … and hope

Wheat is life
for today's bread
to mill and make
to eat and share –
tasting, tasting, fullness … and hope

Wheat is life;
some must be saved
for the children:
tomorrow's world.
Let sacred seed
be cared for;
nurtured deep
in the warm body
of mother earth,
  waiting, waiting
  for sun's warm kiss
  rain's gentle caress.
  Then
bursting, bursting with fullness … and hope.

Joy Mead

Seed is Sacred

In India farmers exchange seed through a beautiful ceremony at the beginning of the growing season. The ceremony is a symbol of recognition that seed is not a private resource – it is a common resource; that seed is not an economic commodity, it is a gift you exchange freely amongst each other. And seed is not just a gift between humans, it is a gift from nature. You have to remember that the multiple exchange between nature and people, and people and people, at every point in time is the basis of sustainable agriculture.

So the seed in India is becoming a symbol of freedom. The movement against seed patenting is the Movement for Seed Freedom, the Seed Satyagraha.

Bere

Since people came to live permanently in the Orkneys they have grown grain – four-row barley, called *Bere*, not so productive but much more hardy than our modern two-row variety. This native grain comes from the middle East and must have been traded between peoples across Europe.

When modern ideas with other grains came here Orcadians were accused of being unwilling to adopt newer ways. But farming on the edge of the grain-growing world, where margins are small, you had to use the system you knew gave returns. If the new ideas worked that was excellent, but if not, starvation stared you in the face. Best work with what had always brought results, so corn (bere) lingered on in Orkney for bread and malt are symbols of life and hope.

Peter Leith

Seedlings

There is a very simple and meaningful practice among the woefully underpaid farm labourers of Tamil Nadu, India.

Rice is the staple food for the people of Tamil Nadu. The seed form of rice with its husk is called paddy. Paddy is cultivated in wet fields. It is first sown thickly in a small plot of land. The seedlings are then transplanted in well spaced rows in another larger field made wet and muddy.

Little girls from the families of those at work will go to the road and nearby streets with small bunches of seedlings in their hands. They will place them at the feet of the passers-by, and, with the left hand pointing to the fields where the work is in progress, will stretch out the right hand and ask for a small donation. Many people will just give a few coins, often cursing the urchins for resorting to begging: the real meaning of this 'begging' has eluded them.

The meaning, however, was made known by one little girl. A passer-by scolded her for taking to begging. She faced him courageously and retorted that she was not a beggar. She asked the man to look at the fields where many women were standing in a bent posture in ankle deep wet mud and were involved in transplanting the seedlings. She then told the man that they were working in order that he could be fed and sustained. Having thus made the man aware of his heavy indebtedness to these people who were so poorly paid, she then demanded with great dignity that he give her a handsome donation …

The challenge to remember all the underpaid and unpaid labour with a grateful heart is great – and was indeed the reason behind the practice.

Bread is made of God's gifts in nature – rain, fertility of soil, and seed. But it is also made with human labour. The sweat of toil is a constituent element of bread. Our Lord seems to have wanted people, in the eucharist, to become aware how, in ordinary bread, God and human labour were united in a process of self-giving to sustain life.

Dhyanchand Carr

Harvest

Those who sow in tears
will reap with songs of joy.
He who goes out weeping
carrying his bag of seed
will come back with songs of joy
carrying home his sheaves.
(Psalm 126)

Waving wheat
and dancing feet;
wooing of earth
gathering grain
and people;
bringing home sheaves
with music and laughter
gathering time
and memory.

Lugh, god of harvest-time,
sits so lightly to life
he has been known
to dance on a bubble
without bursting it.

His celebration
is music and movement,
rhythm of seasons;
sowing and harvest;

wordless; fragile
as that bubble:
yet as enduring
as a heart
of uncrushable joy. *

Joy Mead

*Lughnasa, the festival of Lugh the Celtic god of the
harvest, was so important in the lives of the people of
Ireland and so involved with their ideas of welfare that
Christianity had to adopt it or permit it to survive.

Quern Questions

No one may take millstones,
or even the upper millstones alone, in pledge;
that would be taking a life in pledge.
Deut 24:6

Quern* is a word
for every season's fire,
for day and night,
sunrise and sunset
the year's cycle
the moon's cycle.
It is a word to challenge
abstractions for always:
a question embodied

in the hardness of stone
and the softness of grain;
in the way life's sweetness
is squeezed out;
in the way these stones
may not be taken
in pledge.
For if you lose your millstones
your life is taken.
The stones you know
will be in at the end.

Joy Mead

*A rotary mill – at first with thick stones of small diameter, but later querns were neater and lighter.

Think about the effect of debt repayments on economically poor countries and you will realise that we, the economically rich, have 'taken the millstones in pledge'.

Ulva Millstones

On the far shore of an island
where to look is healing,
I pause
sensing that I have arrived;
looking for somewhere to rest
my eyes.

At my feet
disused and discarded
are two massive millstones,
moss-covered, almost hidden,
cradled in nettles,
perfectly at home.

They guard the essence
of their story
circling the unsaid
centre which is sustenance
in this place of regeneration
where there are ghosts
of bread.

Joy Mead

Women and Millstones

(Numbers 11:8)

When Moses led the Israelite slaves
out of Egypt, the women
took their millstones
not as a weight
around their necks
but as heart and hearth
of home: the means
to make the manna
of their dreams
into the bread
of life.

Joy Mead

Ulva*

Above rocks so old
they make the millennium meaningless
ravens are good and bad angels.**
They circle a story that tells
how once they brought the bread
to sustain body and imagination;
how once they picked the bones clean.

In the intense quiet –
the sound of the mill wheel
is an echo in our minds
only – and the shades
that touch us
are the toiling of long ago people.

The isle is a place of sealed hunger;
full of the whisperings
of a community destroyed;
land stolen; food stolen.
Now, it seems, only the stones
wait to cry out
when the fishers come.

Water baptises this place;
washes down
beside the resting mill stones.
These great circles
once cracked wheat grains
letting out a life-giving sweetness
to be tenderly touched
with sweaty, salty hands.
Earth and breath, water –
the first gift – and fire
make the one loaf:
warm and gold, brown and round
set upon a winter table
to be broken and shared
noisily; consecrated
in hungry mouths,
in homely communion;
taste on the tongue;
story on the tongue;
bread for today's eating
and something to save
for tomorrow.

Joy Mead

* Ulva is an island off the north-west coast of
Mull, with a landscape forged by fire and ice,
rocks about 60 million years old, stunning
scenery and some hauntingly evocative ruins.

**Ravens, strange angels, bringers of light and
dark, good and evil, bread and death.

Refugee

Roasted grains offered
into open hands:
water shared; bread broken
… in harmony with each other
and with God's good earth
which fed them all
in this man's
fertile land.

She had come from afar
seeking this place of refuge,
carrying her own suffering,
her hunger … and her story
deep inside her.

'Why,' she asked the good man
from Bethlehem
'are you so kind
as to notice me
a stranger in your land.'

'Come,' he said. 'I have heard
your story; you are stranger
no longer; come and eat
the fruit of my fields.
There is bread between us.'

Story in her;
story in him;
difference joyfully shared,

... pieces picked up
like broken grain
and kneaded gently
to make a new story
to change the world.

Joy Mead

Bread and Music

An Orkney story tells of two fiddlers walking home from a wedding. Passing a knoll, or burial mound, one turns to answer the other's question. His companion has gone.

Some years later, the fiddler left behind is again walking the same road. He turns and sees his former companion once more on the road with him and looking not an hour older than when he disappeared.

The story tells that he had been taken by the earth energies that bring to life grass and grain. They had stolen his music to make the wheat grow tall and golden under the summer sun.

Blessed be the God who puts song and dance at the heart of all life.

Joy Mead

This song arises out of the experience of women in the Horn of Africa. It reveals some insights of those engaged in both harvesting and household tasks, but whose voices are rarely heard.

Hear me, my grains, my grains of wheat –
while I tell my tale.
When we brought you from the harvest fields
you filled the basket to the brim;
but after all that labour on the land,
when you come to the grindstone,
instead of ten donkey-loads,
you are only a few handfuls.
The feudals have taken it all.

My hands, hear me as you grind,
hear me and take care
not to let fall the smallest grain
and waste it on the floor.
The Lady in the feudal's house
sits idle, with her hands
adorned with gold and henna.
But my hands are ground down
with work, and fighting
with this stone –
to ward off hunger.

Song of Communion

Let's go to the corn patch
to the supper of the Lord
Jesus Christ is inviting
to his harvest of love
the cornfields shine
in the sunlight
let's go to the supper
of communion.

**Carlos Jejia Godoy and
Pablo Martinez, Nicaragua**

A Hymn on Not Giving Up

Were the world to end tomorrow,
would we plant a tree today?
Would we till the soil of loving,
kneel to work and rise to pray?

Dare we try and give an answer,
reaching out in fragile hope,
touching lives with words of Easter,
break a loaf and share a cup?

Born into the brittle morning
of that final earthy day,
would we be intent on seeing
Christ in others on our way?

Pray that at the end of living,
of philosophies and creeds,
God will find the people busy
planting trees and sowing seeds.

Fred Kaan

God of small beginnings
and rising hopes,
may we see eternity
in each wheat grain:
ours for today's bread
and tomorrow's planting;
food of life; gift to the future
and seed of hope.

Joy Mead

Part Two

Salt, Time and Broken Grain ...
The Quiet Mystery

Bread is sensual. It requires soft touch. Look closely at your hands. There is where you will learn the mysteries of breadmaking: by experiencing fleshiness and form, shape and warmth. The wonder is in our own hands. Breadmaking can make us aware of goodness and joy in creating, shaping and sharing. We learn some of earth's secrets; it's all about life and living. In the meeting of earth in broken grain and spirit through the hands of the maker/baker, bread becomes the balancing point of all life. 'Jesus seems to have wanted people in the eucharist to become aware how, in ordinary bread, God and human labour were united in a process of self-giving to sustain life.'[1]

It's good to be a maker (see p.83). Everyone seems to understand the mystery and harmony of bread, the unity of spiritual and material, 'breath into dough'. The more we think about the bread we eat the more aware we become of our roots in the soil from which all bread comes, of belonging to the earth; of the oneness of spirit and senses. The material and the making are inseparable from the mystery. Moses in the desert prayed to God for bread – and was given a mystery: 'What is it? Manna' (see Part 3). The raven is a dark bird of mystery, portentous, symbolising evil, the devil, and yet it is identified with Lugh, the Celtic god of the harvest, and provides in unexpected places, bringing bread to Elijah: 'You will be fed by ravens in the desert'[2] – showing us how intertwined all things are

Soft touch ... and then ... time and timelessness. Breadmaking is a slow process needing patience, quietness, a sense of mystery, an aware-ness of hidden activity. Yeast itself is mysterious. It is a living, growing plant yet its deathly smell evokes a sense of the necessary naturalness of decay, rotting, dying, in the cycle of all things. Have we, I wonder, lost touch with bread? Has it gone from staple to a food envelope? Has it been adapted to the impatience of an industrialised world? What about 'no-time' dough – can there be such a thing? Yeast lives, grows and dies for the finished bread and there is something inexplicably joyful about a rising loaf. Perhaps it's to do with spontaneity and resurrection. Natural yeasts used in old sourdough recipes appear spontaneously out of the unity of wheat and air. Try some. Using them is an interesting experience. Sourdough has something of wheat's own immortality. It is often handed down through generations – part of a culture always saved for tomorrow … in food … in hopes and dreams. Bread is made with love and for those who love, time is eternity: a losing of oneself in the larger dream, the larger whole:

And so the kingdom comes, he said
In hidden ferment of the yeast,
In vagrants summoned to a feast,
In broken bread:
What's undervalued in its place
Is charged with grace.[3]

Have a go at making some bread. It may change your life!

1 Dyanchand Carr, India, from *Dare to Dream*, ed. Geoffrey Duncan (Fount, London, 1995, p.214) © Christian Conference of Asia: from 'Patterns of Witness in the Midst of Religious Plurality, CCA News July/August 1993
2 1 Kings 17:4
3 John Bell, The Iona Community, from 'The Greatness of the Small' in *Love From Below* (Wild Goose Publications, 1989, p.62)

Beginnings

Once, a long time ago
on a warm sunny day
a mixture of meal and water,
waiting to be parched
on hot stones
or boiled into paste or gruel,
was left longer than usual
before baking.

While the woman was away
doing something else
time, moisture and warmth
set a sourdough mystery
into action.

So, from then onwards
hard, stubborn grain cakes,
holding hidden yeasts,
become the wonder
we call bread.

——

Maybe in the days
when beer and bread
were created
out of the one place,
a jug of ale
fell into a kneading trough
and while things went on

elsewhere, there began
a magic moment,
a process of transformation,
a ferment, that made baked dough
good to eat – made the wonder
of bread.

Joy Mead

Out of the Everywhere
(**Matthew** 13:33)

In the beginning
is the yeast.
This quietest of all possibilities
lives on leaves and tree bark,
in soil and on fruit skins,
in seed and fresh air,
comes from the everywhere.

A woman, the storyteller
of long ago Palestine
tells us, takes this yeast,
and adds to it
three measures of flour.
Tended by time
and a woman's caring
hands, the yeast begins

its all pervasive activity.
Quietly, gently, it renews,
enlarges, transforms,
irreversibly filling all matter
with anticipation and airiness,
with creative, life-affirming
vitality.

The storyteller sits butterfly light
to life. He makes water into wine
to give the party sweetness
and flavour. He celebrates
the beauty of bread;
pictures its sensual
sculptural, visual pleasure;
touches the moment
when the prospect of a hard grain cake
becomes the possibility
that satisfies
belly, spirit and senses:
the full-bodied
breadiness of bread: purity
in wholeness and joy:
the livingness of life.

And the yeast
holds on to its mystery.

Joy Mead

Secret Bread

Come: experience bread –
in the making: a slow art, needing
time to love and to touch.
Imagine: response and warmth –
the soft fleshiness
of the dough in your hands
gently moulding, giving shape
and contour.

Let the richness
of the moist, earthy smell
penetrate you wholly.
It is the smell of our roots,
the earth's fragrance,
and carries the gentle life
and death secrets
of grain that dies
deep in the dark
of a winter field
then lives again
in a sun-drenched field
of immortal wheat.

Ripe grains are gathered,
cracked and milled
their sweetness liberated
to mingle with the salt taste,
of hands after work –
the taste in your mouth
the memory of a kiss.

Wait: knowing all this
for the soft-bellied rising

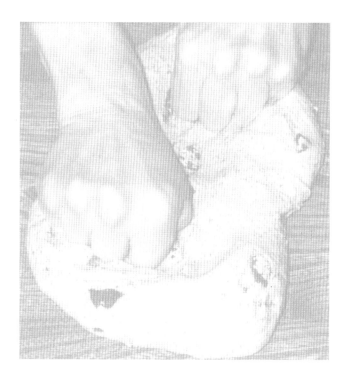

of the loaves; happening
while you're doing something else
going on without you – unstoppable.

Then the age-old process
of baking – smells of home
and welcome
in breaking and sharing –
the grainy taste in your mouth;
memory – and joy
in the wholeness
of this moment.

All things in this thing;
our earth we eat
together

Joy Mead

Martha

(Luke 10:38–42; 13:20–21)

I'm Martha.
I baked the bread –
what do you think I was doing
in the kitchen?
I took yeast
mixed it with flour
left it to rise.
I'm wise enough to know
that bread can't be hurried.
But it was later,
when I was kneading the dough
and Mary was listening to Jesus –
because just then she felt that
was what she needed to do –
when my hands were full
of the sticky, clinging dough,
that I saw the fire going out
in the bake oven in the yard
and I called out
'Mary – come and help!'
Daily bread needs hands.

Jan Sutch Pickard

Bread

Towards the end of our holiday in northern France we happened upon a 'Chambre d'Hôte' which was a working farm. It was mainly dairy, but the two daughters of the house were also setting up an educational project that involved renovating some derelict buildings to their original purpose and plan. They had decided to start with the old bakehouse, and we'd arrived on the very day that they were celebrating its inauguration. A dozen friends were coming to help light the fire, to bake the bread and flans and pizzas, and to celebrate the breaking of the first bread. We were welcome to join in, they said. So we did. The warm fresh bread that evening was dusted with ash that hadn't quite been swept from the oven floor, but washed down with the local wine and perry it was crusty and delicious.

A few weeks later I took part in a Lammas celebration that included the baking and sharing of bread. In the morning we kneaded the dough into different shapes before it was carried off to the oven to be baked. In the evening we sat round a bonfire in a huge field and shared it. This time we didn't wash it down with drink but we digested it with singing and dancing. One of my sandals had broken as I climbed over the stile, so I threw them both off and danced barefoot, avoiding thistles and cowpats where I could. This bread, too, spread with butter that was crumby from everyone else's buns and well flavoured with smoke from the fire, was scrumptious.

The Christians knew from the beginning that there was something symbolic about bread. It is the basic foodstuff. 'Bread' means, idiomatically, what we live on, and so, by extension, money or gifts or the spirit of life. I started baking my own bread years ago, shamed into it by a friend with twin toddlers and a part-time job who I found kneading dough in the kitchen when the kids were asleep. 'It doesn't take much work,' she said. 'You just have to be around for a few hours. What it mostly needs is patience.' My early efforts would have been better as bricks in the garden wall than as breakfast on the table, but the results improved markedly when I followed a good recipe and now I can do it without thinking.

But I'm sure my bread tastes better when I *am* thinking: when I'm taking pleasure in the sugary yeast mixture as it bubbles up, when I'm aware of the physical and spiritual energy I'm putting into every shove and thump as I knead, when I marvel at the alchemy of the rising dough, when I smile as I breathe in the heavenly smell of the loaves as they're tapped out of their tins.

'Bread of heaven, Bread of heaven,' I used sing as an eager little girl in the school choir, 'Feed me now and ever more.' Those celebrations of making and breaking the bread, for party and for harvest, nourished me through my senses of smell and of taste, through the grain of the good earth, the heat of fire and the oven, and through the warmth of friendly communion.

Alison Leonard

Good To Be a Breadmaker

A meditation on activity and ingredients

Making bread is an elemental activity needing in the right proportions:

earth, that is statement and naming, and soil for bearing plants;
air, that is rising and transforming, that is breathing and taking words to make them grow, that knows no frontiers; that is shared.
water, that is a quest, a flowing, a search, that is about waves of energy and lakes of stillness. Water, at the temperature of your own body. If it is hotter it will kill the yeast.
fire so deeply embodied in the wonder of creation, that is about the energy to rise, to love; about the doing of bread, what happens around a fire: a meal cooked and shared, stories shared; the command to rise, in the fullness of time.

Being a breadmaker is a good and poetic way to be. It needs time and love. It puts us back in touch with our roots, makes us aware of the sacredness of our earth and its gifts. These are the stuff of bread and poetry, bringing their own stories to the one story, the many ingredients to the one loaf:

Flour – the sweetness of cracked grain, milled from sunlight.
Oil – for tenderness and moistness.
Flour and oil: these are the men's gifts.
Water – the first gift, flowing through all life, reminding us we are one.
Yeast – a plant with a single cell, putting out buds and making more buds – an ever recurring mystery, needing love and care; a living organism, growing on beer, coming naturally, spontaneously out of the air and from the wheat itself to make sourdough, the culture saved from yesterday's baking. Sourdough bread is the oldest recipe in history preserved through generations.
Salt – to enhance flavour and slow the activity of yeast; to hold a mystery – a way to remember the many salt tears we weep for home; salt in the sweat of hands that have touched the earth, hands that labour and love.
A little milk – the product of the mother, to give life
A little honey – to give love of life, for good-to-be-alive sweetness and tenderness. Honey tells of a world of sufficiency and sharing. Milk and honey: these are the women's gifts.
Sweat – for this milk and honey land is no dream of luxury, of fleshpots and doing nothing; no fool's paradise. It is a dream of life based on natural resources, of fertility and natural order, of honest toil and the sweat of moist hands that shape and feel as they knead together different elements
Time – love of life and our good earth involves patience, makes time an eternity of warm breath, sweet hours … and waiting … guiding the dough … making suggestions, not forcing … waiting until the texture is flesh-like, springy and alive. Breadmaking is a slow art.

Joy Mead

Joy's Recipe

350 g organic wholemeal flour

350 g organic strong white flour

(Use a good, well-flavoured flour – I suggest Doves Farm or Shipton Mill)

15 g salt

430 ml water and milk mixed – lukewarm

15 g fresh yeast

1 tsp honey

Oil

1 large loaf tin – If you go to Denmark try to get hold of an Evan Slip Let Rye Bread tin. This is a professional baking tin used throughout Europe. If you touch the 'slip let' layer inside the tin it is cold and dry and feels like rubber. When it is warm and moist it becomes so smooth that the bread slides effortlessly out of the tin. It is recommended for rye bread but I use mine for all kinds of yeast-doughs.

To make your bread:

Mix flours and salt

Dissolve yeast in a little milk/water; make a well in the flours and add dissolved yeast and rest of liquid

Make a batter in the well, cover with flour and leave to 'sponge' for about 20 minutes

Add the honey; mix to a dough and knead for ten minutes

Put in an oiled bowl making sure that the surface of the dough is oiled; cover the bowl loosely with a plastic bag or damp cloth; leave to rise (at normal room temperature) for at least two hours

Knock back the dough for about three minutes; put into a loaf tin; again cover with plastic bag or damp cloth

Leave to rise for about an hour (be careful not to leave the dough too long this time)

Bake in a hot oven: Gas 8 (230C, 450F) for 15 minutes then reduce to 6 (200C, 400F) for 30 minutes.

Adding 25–50 g rye or barley meal gives extra flavour (but your loaf may be slightly heavier). Reduce the amount of flour accordingly.

Abbey Bread

Bread is baked daily in the kitchens of the Abbey and the MacLeod Centre on Iona to be shared in simple meals and in our weekly communion – a bread for heart and soul.

This recipe makes enough for two loaves or will make a large round communion loaf for Sunday. One loaf should be enough for the Friday evening communion.

5 kg malthouse (harvester/granary) flour
4 teaspoons salt
8 sachets dried yeast
200 ml sunflower oil
about 2.5 litres warm water.

Place flour, salt and yeast in the food mixer and stir together using dough hook at no. 1 setting. Add the sunflower oil and water until all the loose flour is absorbed into the dough, without the dough being too sticky. Knead for 5 minutes or so.

Cover the mixing bowl with a tea-towel and leave to rise for an hour or more in the drying room.

Punch the dough down, then knead it once more in the mixer for about 5 minutes. While this is happening, grease ten bread tins thoroughly, and wipe down a space on the table, sprinkling it with flour.

Take the dough out of the mixing bowl and knead it by hand for a minute or so on the table, forming it into a block. Cut this in half with the dough cutter, then cut each half into five equal pieces. Take a piece, knead it flat, roll it up, repeat the action, then press the rolled-up piece into a tin. Repeat this for the other nine loaves, working quickly so that the dough does not go cold.

Place the tins on trays in a warm place, e.g. on the cooker, cover them with tea-towels and leave them for 45 minutes or so until risen.

Bake at Gas 6 (200C, 400F) for 30 minutes, checking them after 20 to see if they need turning round. After 30 minutes turn them out of their tins upside down on to the tray and bake for a further 10–15 minutes, checking them frequently, until the sides and bottom are crisp and the loaves make a hollow sound when drummed.

Turn them on to racks to cool, covered with tea-towels.

Gillian's Recipe

Bara Mêl

This is a lovely breakfast bread, moist and very slightly sweet, good after a morning bowl of fruit, with or without butter, honey, fruit jellies or jams. The dough will take a small handful of seeds, nuts, dried cranberries or papaya. Try my everyday version first, then experiment.

Ingredients:
large bowl for:

1.35 Kg flour:
   half strong brown flour (or white)
   half malted granary flour
teaspoon of salt
75 g sunflower seeds
2 packets of easy-bake yeast

2 pint jug for:
4–5 fluid oz olive oil (around 150 ml)
tablespoon of honey
very hot water added to the pint mark
cold water to the pint and a half mark.
It may need a little more water.

Method:
Put all dry ingredients into the bowl. Pour the liquid in. Mix well to a sticky dough.

Knead on a floured board. Divide into three. Let the dough rise in the tins somewhere warm.

Bake at Gas Mark 5 (190C, 375F) for 25 minutes. The loaves should be brown, should turn out easily, the bottom of the loaf firm if you tap it.

Gillian's poem is on page 75: more information about her books in the recommended reading on page 91.

Lot Bakes for Angels

(Genesis 19)

Two angels come to Lot
sitting at his gate in Sodom.
He offers them shelter
and the gift
of pure, unleavened bread:
food for journeys
and the unexpected;
suitable for visiting angels.

When men come to the gate
asking for the angels
Lot offers his virgin daughters:
'You can do what you like
with them.'
And the food of purity:
where will we eat that?

I wonder about this unleavened bread
tasting of haste and purity
and think how Jesus offers
the Bread of Life:
wholeness and fullness:
rich and yeasty, alive and rising,
love-filled, time-taking, home food –
not pure maybe, but good
because it has the touch
of what it means
to be truly human.

And in the morning
Lot, his wives and daughters
are gone.

Joy Mead

The Spirit of Bread

The spirit of village bread baking began over five thousand years ago when families and small tribes huddled together around the campfire to eat mush. Made from water and crushed grains, the first porridge of gruel had to be eaten immediately. One day, the porridge was accidentally left over the fire and it cooked into a rock-hard cake or galette. Dense and unappealing as it may have been, that primitive bread would last a few more days, heralding the first historic preservation of grains. It also made it easier to carry along on the hunt and into battle.

Still later, that same mush, left out in a warm moist atmosphere, fermented. The result was a bubbly mixture – the original sourdough culture and the first yeast. When this fermented mush was mixed with fresh grain and then baked on a stone over the campfire, it became lighter and more edible: the first leavened bread as we know it.

The evolution of mush is important in the development of the village bakery because it shows us that the mistake that made gruel into bread was also the first real recipe for bread, even though it was just a set of crude proportions based simply on experience. It shows that baking is a natural process that can be guided by someone in order to yield a predictable loaf. Long before there were village bakers, people learned that the craft of bread baking was as organic as that of making wine or cheese. Almost everyone knew the simple, natural time patterns that made up the method. Gradually – over perhaps the first few thousand years – making bread became another task around the house, like maintaining the hearth fire, building the compost mound, or tending the garden. As an ongoing process, it took on a life of its own. Bread had to be watched, guarded, responded to.

Joe Ortiz

Leaven

Yeast and naturally leavened doughs are mysterious – we don't know all there is to know about them. Before the advent of commercial yeast, there was only naturally leavened dough which comes about spontaneously – a mix of flour, water, and air. It has a special flavour and makes a thick, crispy, crusty bread of greater density than a yeast bread with a thick and crispy crust. Its inside is irregular and elastic. It can be cut very thin and has a tangy taste very hard to imitate in a yeast bread.

Long ago soured grains (soaked, left over, cooked, and sprouted) from beer making and the foam from wine vats were added to dough to make the bread rise. This natural leavening takes time but the whole process has a sense of timelessness about it. The bread ages well. In the open it keeps its flavour and moisture inside and its crispness on the outside. Once naturally leavened dough is created a portion must be kept as a starter to introduce into the next baking … always save something for tomorrow …

So the leaven is the story left over from yesterday and carried on to tomorrow. A little of the dough is kept from the last baking (it will keep in the fridge for a month) but if the leaven doesn't work you can start a new one for rye bread with 120 g rye flour, 150 ml buttermilk, $1/2$ tsp salt. Mix together; cover. The leaven is ready to use after 2–3 days at room temperature.

Joy Mead

Bread-time

1
Because bread won't be hurried
we have to learn to let be,
to do nothing, to be patient,
to wait for the proving.
Because bread won't be hurried
and is a life and death process,
we find out in its making
that time is not a line
but a cycle of ends and beginnings
rhythms and seasons,
growth and death,
celebration and mourning,
work and rest,
eating and fasting,
because bread won't be hurried.

2
In a pyramid in Egypt
a few grains of wheat
lay surrounded by death
– dormant for thousands of years.
They waited quietly
until the time was right,
until the life impulse
was awakened by the good earth,
warmed by the sun
and ready to dance
in the bread of tomorrow.

Joy Mead

'... not against baker's leaven'

Paul, it seems, thought
truth and sincerity to be in the history
and purity of unleavened bread.
But wasn't it more
the haste of a people
anxious to leave captivity
and so with no time
to wait for a rising.

I wonder.
Didn't Jesus show us
truth and hope
in the light and lovely
pleasure-making, wholly joy-filled,
god-given, fully-leavened loaf
enjoyed while watching
the flowers of the fields.

Do this, he said
take wine and bread
together
fruit and grain
old customs
old ways.
I make them new
in the irreversible power
of community.

Joy Mead

70

Bread and Time

Summer in the English countryside is enlivened by local competitions, some originating so long ago that the original point of rolling eggs down a hill or batting a piece of wood along winding lanes is lost to most of the participants. About twenty years ago, a new race was started – this time with pointlessness built in. The challenge was to see who could make a loaf of bread quickest, starting with wheat standing in the field and following – after a fashion – all the normal stages of breadmaking. In the early years, the contestants would cut the wheat with a combine, drive the grain to a mill, then rush the flour to a bakery for the mixing, moulding, proving and baking. Times of under an hour were slated. But then it all got out of hand: someone set up a mill and an oven in the middle of a wheat field and claimed a finished loaf in under 25 minutes! Fanfares in the baking press, a handy donation to some good cause and satisfaction for the obligatory sponsor, no doubt. But the bread – if it could be called that – had been robbed of its essence: time. Without time to ferment the dough and allow the micro-organisms to interact, bread not only lacks flavour but may not be the staff of life we fondly imagine.

For the British baking industry in the past fifty or so years, a more serious race has been on: to make mass-produced bread as quickly as possible in the interests of profit and low prices. Most big plants moved to the 'no-time dough', in which a combination of high-speed mixing and chemical additives substituted for traditional fermentation. No-time dough: the very antithesis of leavened bread as it first emerged many thousands of years ago. For we may surmise that it was, above all, time which caused that first left-over piece of flour-and-water dough to surprise its maker by rising a little after a few hours of benign neglect. Wild yeasts in the flour, activated by water and warmth, began to ferment the starches, producing carbon dioxide which inflated the dough. Without time and watchfulness, there would be no bread as we know it.

In the pre-industrial era, time was an essential ingredient in bread-making, even after the processes of fermentation were well understood. Before the advent of commercial yeasts, bakers had to make their own leavening mixture. There were various methods. Barms could be made by fermenting potatoes, barley malt or other suitable carbohydrate in a process similar to brewing; or flour could be mixed with water and left to form a sourdough by the action of wild yeasts and bacteria. Either way, it took days to produce a vigorous 'starter' culture, which, when mixed with flour to form a final dough, would take several hours to produce the necessary fermentation gases to raise the loaf. Even when chemists isolated the strains of the yeast saccharomyces most suitable for bread-making, the resulting product, though highly concentrated, was relatively expensive. Strategies were found to eke it out. Rather than use enough yeast to raise the bread from scratch in a couple of hours, a much smaller amount was mixed into a wet flour-and-water dough called a sponge or ferment. This would be left for several hours (often overnight) until a vigorous fermentation was established and the yeast cells had multiplied many-fold, whereupon they were capable of raising a much larger bulk of dough than earlier in the process. Time not only rewards the patient baker with an economy of raw materials. Something else happens as dough ferments: lactic and acetic acid bacteria start to develop. Over time, in warm conditions, they produce the ripe aroma and slightly tangy taste of well-fermented bread.

If watchfulness brought our first discovery of leavening, patience and care seem to have been integral to most of breadmaking until quick-acting yeast and mechanical power made such values redundant. So universal was the nostrum 'time = money' in the bread business that I was fourteen years into a baking career before I really began to understand how, in fact, wonderful bread needs plenty of time – and not a little love. The circumstances were unusual.

I had studied Russian at university and, fascinated by the language and culture, started a career as a producer in the BBC Russian Service,

making programmes for a Soviet audience denied access to truthful information about Britain and the world. As I tried to understand and report on the incipient environmental crisis of the early 1970s, I felt a pull to live my own life in a more self-reliant, less damaging way. In 1976 I moved to Cumbria to grow my own food and started baking bread to help pay the mortgage. Russia seemed a thing of the past until, out of the blue, I was invited to visit by the brother of a former colleague. Perestroika was on the agenda and Russia was opening up. Sixteen years after my previous visit, I couldn't wait to go. To justify my self-indulgence and mollify the taxman, bakery research was the stated objective. My Russian host took me at my word and when I arrived in the ancient city of Kostroma in 1990, it seemed as though everyone, from bakery manager to passport officer, had heard of my mission to understand Russian bread.

Though I was warmly welcomed at the 100-ton-a-day bread factory, I felt that home breadmakers would be more likely to reveal the secrets of that quintessential sour rye bread which had once kept me alive on a student camping trip to Russia in the 1960s when failure to understand the exchange rate limited our menu to – what else? – the staff of life. So when my Russian friends dropped me at Nina's log cabin in the village of Teterinskoye on a snowy Saturday afternoon in February, I was ready to learn. I expected to watch her make bread there and then and bake it in the big masonry stove which occupied much of the house. But pensioner Nina was in no hurry. First we had to prepare the zakvaska or sourdough, a sloppy mixture of rye flour and water in which both wild yeasts and beneficial lactobacilli would begin to multiply, frothing the dough to the brim of the old enamel mixing bucket. As Nina talked with simple candour of life in a Soviet village from collectivisation to perestroika, I wondered when we would make the dough proper. 'All in good time', she said, with a smile which turned to bemusement when I asked if I could spend the night on top of the stove, in the place traditionally reserved for baboushka, but in this gas-heated cabin now abandoned to two very territorial cats. From my first encounter with the wood-fired pechka in 19th-century literature, it had seemed that to sleep on even its lower ledges would symbolise acceptance into the heart and hearth of Mother Russia. Any such romantic notions were progressively dispelled by the hard surface, suffocating heat and partisan raids by the displaced pets. Mercifully, breadmaking resumed at 4 am: the final stages had to be started before church. The overnight sourdough had dropped back from its frothy peak and now smelled distinctly fruity, with a hint of vinegar. We added more rye flour, a thick black malt, water and a little salt and dropped the soft sticky dough into greased round tins. Nina smoothed the surface with a wet hand before making the sign of the cross over each loaf in a traditional gesture which perhaps combines hope of 'enlighten-ment' (for the bread) and thankfulness for impending nourishment.

We covered the tins with a damp cloth and set off down a snowy ravine to church. The significance of time is not lost on the Orthodox liturgy and more than three hours later we shuffled back to the cabin to find our bread nearly risen. The fire which Nina had set first thing in the morning had done its work. A quick scuffle of the oven floor to remove the cinders and in went the bread. An hour later, as Nina tipped the loaves out of the tins, tapped their bases and declared them done, my friends arrived to take me back to Kostroma. It was nearly twenty hours from start to finish and the warm loaf I cradled in my lap as we bounced over ice-rutted tracks brought home the link between patience and reward, time and real value.

For a sourdough system such as Nina's to work, a vigorous starter dough is needed. A small portion can be kept back each baking day and 'refreshed' with flour and water to begin the next batch. So some of the original brew of wild yeasts and bacteria would be transmitted to later doughs. It was this fact which encouraged me to accept the Kostroma bakery's offer of a piece of their rye sourdough in 1990. Refreshed and used almost every day since then, it has leavened over two million Village Bakery rye loaves in the past decade.

In Russia, it was common in peasant households for a young woman leaving home to get married to smear her new breadmaking pancheon with some of her mother's zakvaska to ensure that subsequent genera-tions of dough would 'breed true' and make well-risen, tasty bread. Thus the baking of bread, far from being a one-off batch process dependent on yeast manufactured by microbiologists, is a never-ending cascade in which the leavening life-force is passed on and renewed through time.

Sourdoughs or leavens (the words are pretty interchangeable), in which time plays such a vital role, have other advantages besides economy and flavour. The action of the lactobacillus bacteria partially 'pre-digests' some of the starches in the flour, rendering the bread more digestible. Moisture retention and keeping quality are significantly better than in quickly made yeasted breads. Furthermore, in wholemeal or higher fibre breads, the sourdough process generates an enzyme –

phytase – which neutralises the phytic acid which otherwise tends to prevent the uptake of calcium and magnesium by the human digestive system.

In modern commercial baking, there is pressure to make bread fast. Yeast is relatively cheap, so it 'pays' to use more. It is possible that excess yeast may not be fully fermented in a quick dough, leaving residues in baked bread which may progressively affect the gut flora. Is it any wonder that more and more people appear to be suffering from allergies to yeast?

Modern distribution systems, dedicated to provide multiple retailers with maximum freshness, interrupt the rhythm of time necessary to real bread. So we get 'bake-off', a generic term for giving a quick hot final 'bake' to bread which has been made and either part-baked or frozen unbaked at some earlier juncture. French bakers were so outraged by such violations of the breadmaking process that they succeeded in getting a law passed limiting the title *boulangerie* to places in which the five essential stages were completed in one uninterrupted time frame: mixing, fermenting, moulding, proving, baking.

Perhaps the failure to accord bread its rightful time is part of our modern cult of youth and the consumerist desire to replicate pleasurable experiences ad nauseam. You like it fresh, madam? Well then, have it fresh – hot, even – every day. We'll put some 'improvers' and 'flour treatment agents' in – as well as some enzymes that, thank goodness, we don't have to declare on the label – and your bread will stay 'fresh' for a whole week!

The trouble is that if absolute freshness (even the ersatz freshness of a 'baked-off' loaf) becomes our minimum standard, we progressively rob ourselves of the benchmark by which the true delight of freshness can be judged. Cream on top of the milk is a treat because it is richer and tastier. Try drinking only cream and you make yourself sick.

When bread was a vital source of sustenance, it was usually so hard won that throwing it away was a sin. Bread (like people) should grow old with dignity. Time unquestionably hardens the starches in baked bread. So we use it in different ways, dunking it in soup, toasting it, covering it trencher-style with succulent stews. Even when quite stale it still delights us, in summer pudding, croûtons or kvass.

Bread teaches us in so many ways that fulfilment follows effort and real nourishment needs patience and time. What price, then, instant gratification? As the old lady said, having queued at the new in-store bakery counter only to find that she was being asked to pay more for hot bread: 'Oh, I'll wait until it cools down, then.' One of the joys of making bread is the opportunity to participate in a whole process whereby simple ingredients are transformed into a baked loaf. It is no surprise that the language of bread finds echoes in religious metaphor. From the germination of the good seed to symbolic identification with the body of Christ, bread speaks to us of becoming, of transformation. And that, it seems to me, takes time.

Andrew Whitley
The Village Bakery Melmerby Ltd
Winner of the Cakes Category, The Organic Food Awards 1999
Winner of the Organic Trophy, 1998
(for more about Andrew see p 156)

Are the People of Moscow Going to Heaven?

Nor do I believe that they have hunger enough
who when they have coarse bread,
still wait for bread that is white and refined.

Pelagius

The food inspector comes,
searching for impurities;
looks up at pigeons
perching on girders
above Andrei Shurkhovetsky,
Baker of Moscow;
sees them shit
into his bread;
sees the roughness
of his kneading room,
and the way cement dust
rolls with the dough
in his loving hands;
watches the sweat of his labour
moisten the bread;
feels his spirit enliven the rising
and his whole life
flow into 200 tonnes of good bread
every day: 'Baking is a calling.
You have to put your soul into it.'

The food inspector blesses

Andrei Shurkhovetsky's bread;
will not discard
bread that is good
but not quite pure
for the city is poor now
and breadwinners wait
silent and hungry
from dawn until late;
wait for the good bread
that brings hope
to all who eat.

The food inspector leaves
with quiet awareness, knowing
the people of Moscow will not die
from eating bad bread;
knowing they will not live
without this baker's promise
of good bread broken for all
at a feast in heaven.

Joy Mead

Note:
A Russian proverb says:

When a Russian dies
the weight of all the bread
he or she has discarded is calculated.
If it is greater than his or her weight
he or she is sent to Hell.

Living Bread

Knowing bread
is knowing the whole round
of life – shaped
from wood and roots,
bodies of dead animals
peat and grass
water and honey sweetness,
the best of earth's gifts
shaped into fleshiness,
so that we wonder
at its softness:
how it smells like us
salty and moist, good
for one last deathlike gesture
oven burial, home to warmth

then joy in the rising
the finished loaf
our own becoming.

We are what we eat.

Joy Mead

... Maker of Heaven and Earth ...

It is a good thing to be a maker.
Breadmaker, pounding breath into dough
on a flat stone;
cake-maker, for celebrations, or chocolate
for times of indulgent misery;
dressmaker, cutting, patterning, fashioning,
fitting to a shape;
toolmaker, the maker's maker;
love-maker, skill-sharing artisan of
pleasure, trust, delight;
baby-maker.

Wood and words, stone and steel,
clay, lace, brick, flower, flour, microchip –
whatever the medium,
it is a good thing to be a maker.
Substantial,
material,
concrete,
the exchange of energies
changing the world.

It is a *great* thing to be a
maker of heaven and earth,
is it not?

Kathy Galloway

Loving God, take our hands
take our lives,
ordinary as wheat or cornmeal,
daily as bread –
our stumbling generosity,
our simple actions,
and find them good enough
to help prepare the feast
for all your people.

Amen

(Christian Aid)

Spirit of Lightness and Life

be with all makers and dreamers:

all who make bread
   and long to share it;
all who make music
   and long to dance;
all who make words
   and long for poetry;
all who are born in flesh
   and long to be human;
all who make love
   and trust their longing
            for life.

Joy Mead

A hymn for all makers:

Communion Calypso

Let us talents and tongues employ,
reaching out with a shout of joy:
bread is broken, the wine is poured,
Christ is spoken and seen and heard.
Jesus lives again, earth can breathe again,
pass the Word around: loaves abound!

Christ is able to make us one,
at the table he set the tone,
teaching people to live to bless,
love in word and in deed express.
Chorus

Jesus calls us in – sends us out
bearing fruit in a world of doubt,
gives us love to tell, bread to share:
God (Immanuel!) everywhere
Chorus

Fred Kaan

Part Three

Priests of the Moment

How can the eucharists we used to find
in all our food have shrunk so fast [1]

I think it was the Russian theologian and philosopher Nicholay Berdyaev who said, 'Bread for me is a material concern but for me in relation to my neighbour's need, it is a spiritual concern.' And the German mystic and theologian, Meister Eckhart, said something along the lines that there is no such thing as my bread, all bread is ours. In the Egypt of 2300 BC to give bread was such a noble, good and saintly thing to do that they used the symbol for bread in the hieroglyphic expression 'to give'. This mysterious food becomes real and achieves its true purpose only when loved, broken and shared (a bit like the toy rabbit in Margery Williams's children's story: *The Velveteen Rabbit* [2]).

What have we done to bread? We have, as David Scott's poem on page 90 tells, come a long way from its ordinary earthiness, its yeasty smell of a damp woodland, or the way in the making it feels and smells like flesh – like death sometimes. Often, we make little sanitised squares or wafers that look nothing like bread and these we share at a meal to remember the man who stood by the shore saying, 'Come and have breakfast' (see p.110). Does disguised, unearthly bread somehow make it easier for us to ignore those with whom we don't share our loaf. In the end, our tables, fridges, cupboards, bakers, tell us as much about worship and where God is as our churches, ministers and altars. Passing bread from hand to hand at ordinary meals – that is the lost art, the sharing, the kitchen eucharist, the whole-life image. The last supper (see my poem p.129), breakfast by the lake (p.110), the meal after the walk on the road to Emmaus (Jan's poem, p.108) – ordinary bread made whole and holy in the sharing. Our stumbling generosity, our simple actions are good enough to prepare a feast for all people.

Serving one another bread is glimpsing life's heart – let us not forget that. When the bread is broken the hands of the one holding the loaf part and her arms are open to share food and life. Bread gives in each step of its creation: to the one who makes and touches and waits; to the one who breaks and serves; to the one who receives and eats. Then this precious vehicle of life is eaten and becomes, somehow, us. So the cycle continues. The God that was there in immortal wheat is there in sharing bread. Isn't this what the Eucharist symbolises: that all meals are sacred; all food is holy; that companionship is sharing the promise of life and strength.

Jesus chose bread as a special sign – solid, smelly, grainy, earthy bread – and initiated a spirituality of ordinariness we might experience in a bread shop (p.140) or kitchen (p.111). In breaking bread at a table with friends all distinctions between holy and common, sacred and secular, material and spiritual are erased:

It is easy to make of love
these ceremonials. As priests
we fold cloth, break bread, share wine,
hope there's enough to go round

....

(The recipe for my best bread
half granary meal, half strong brown flour,
water, sugar, yeast and salt,
is copied out in the small black book)[3]

There *is* enough to go around, you know … but we've got it stored in our freezers. What does that make of our responsibility to give bread not stones? (See p.103)

Bread is only the bread of life if my neighbour passes it to me. The only true way to bless bread is to share it – with all.

And God said:
All shall eat of the earth
All shall eat of the seed
All shall eat of the grain
All shall eat of the harvest
All shall eat of the bread
All shall eat of the power [4]

All shall eat and know the wonder, the miracle: God willing to be known in the celebration of the small and ordinary things of the earth from sacred seed to sharing bread.

1 Christina Whitehead, from 'Horrible Gardens' in *The Garden of Slender Trust* (Bloodaxe Books, 1999, p.9)

2 Margery Williams, *The Velveteen Rabbit,* illustrations by William Nicholson (William Heinemann Ltd, 1922)

3 Gillian Clarke, 'Letter from a far country' in the book of the same title (Carcanet Press, Manchester, 1987, p.12/13)

4 Carter Heywood, from 'Blessing the Bread – A Litany' in *Women's Prayer Service* (Twenty-Third Publications, Mystic, Connecticut, 1987, p.22)

A Long Way from Bread

1

We have come so far from bread.
Rarely do we hear the clatter of the mill wheel;
see the flour in every cranny,
the shaking down of the sack, the chalk on the door,
the rats, the race, the pool,
baking day, and the old loaves:
cob, cottage, plaited, brick.

We have come so far from bread.
Once the crock said 'BREAD'
and the bread was what was there,
and the family's arm went deeper down each day
to find it, and the crust was flavoured.

We have come so far from bread.
Terrifying is the breach between wheat and table,
wheat and bread, bread and what goes for bread.
Loaves come now in regiments, so that loaf
is not the word. Hlaf
is one of the oldest words we have.

2

I go on about bread
because it was to bread
that Jesus trusted
the meaning he had of himself.
It was an honour for bread
to be the knot in the Lord's handkerchief

reminding him about himself. So,
O bread, breakable;
O bread, given;
O bread, a blessing;
count yourself lucky, bread.

3

Not that I am against wafers,
especially the ones produced under steam
from some hidden nunnery
with our Lord crucified into them.
They are at least unleavened, and fit the hand,
without remainder, but it is still
a long way from bread.
Better for each household to have its own bread,
daily, enough and to spare,
dough the size of a rolled towel,
for feeding angels unawares.
Then if the bread is holy,
all that has to do with bread is holy:
board, knife, cupboard,
so that the gap between all things is closed
in our attention to the bread of the day.

4

I know that
'man cannot live on bread alone'.
I say, let us get the bread right.

David Scott

Manna, Meaning What Is it?

There was a sort of whisper,
at first reminding me of the locusts,
a whisper, a wonder, a terrible distinction,
and instantly I thought of the flies and the darkness,
the frogs, the hailstones, the blood, the dying cattle,
the gnats, the boils, and the awesome screaming of the first-born
as the angel of death swept through the land
and our doorstops smeared with the sacrificial blood that made us safe
at least for that moment, before the desert years,
not knowing then remembering, all in patches,
the vast sea itself parting and the chariots drowning,
Yahweh, bondage, delivery, slavery, freedom

and this morning desert on every side
and the people grumbling, my wife and child hungry
remembering the pots of sweet meat in Egypt
and the way we gathered in our tents at evening
singing songs, telling of Joseph, hearing of Abraham
laying claim to the promised land, the place my father called Zion,
where we, the Israelites, would feed off the fat of the land
playing harps, engaged in story, singing songs
even as old Moses did the other day and Miriam with the tambourines
and the children dancing down where the wood burned
and the women crooning as they nursed the babes at breast
before this hunger came and the endless stretches of sand
and all I hear outside is an unchanging question, manna,
meaning what is it, what is it, what is it, what is it –
what is it that the people, the chosen ones, are now wondering at,
the great mystery that they don't understand,

this new thing that has come before their morning eyes:
perhaps springs of water have erupted in the desert,
perhaps Jacob, or his angel, has wandered through the camp,
perhaps Moses was right, and bread has indeed rained down:

I go outside
and the desert is a white frost,
thin flakes of frost covering the hot sand:
manna? The people ask, and I also wonder:
what is this thin frost that covers the desert sand.

I step out
past Moses, beyond Joshua into the promised land,
thin flakes of frost covering the hot sand – manna?
What is this
that slouches towards Bethlehem, this new Jerusalem
this King on a donkey, these crosses, this fire,
this new covenant, this new frost, this new delivery,
this fresh Exodus.

What is the meaning
of this vast desert morning
and a million of our people, the delivered ones,
asking what it is,
this white thing that looks like coriander seed and tastes like
honey.

How easy it is to mock,
to wonder at the atrocities of Vietnam,
the stupidities of the trenches,
the folly of yesterday,
to confine everything to myth and

the wonder of this morning when the dew rose
and nothing but cold whiteness blanketed the land
I was not exempt from asking what it was.

What is this star,
these fabled shepherds old in story,
this swaddled child in a manger,
this man who healed the sick,
this stranger being whipped,
this cross, this tomb, this controversy:
what is this white frost on the ground,
this old story out of Jewish history,
this morning's sunshine, this clock, this hour,
this night in Edinburgh, this breath, saying

'I went to church last Sunday
and I heard the minister preaching:
"I am the bread of life" he said:
"and he who comes to me will never go hungry." '
And I saying now after the Exodus and the cross,
'I believe': this white thing is manna,
this thin frost is bread, this thing is atonement,
white frost, coriander seed, honey sweet, a life.

Angus Peter Campbell

The Children of Israel
(Exodus 16:2–20)

Why?
we asked, the children of Israel
wandering in the wilderness
wondering in the wilderness,
questioning everything,
complaining to Moses.
Why did you bring us out of Egypt?
We had plenty of bread there.
Why did you bring us here to starve?

What?
we asked, what is all this
about bread from heaven?
Have you passed on our complaints?
How can even God feed us here
in this God-forsaken place?
We accuse you, Moses
and we're asking God – Why?

When?
we asked. When will we be fed?
'Between dusk and dark meat to eat
and in the morning bread in plenty.'
Why then? Why to us?
Who will deliver the goods?
What makes this time and place
different from any other time –

anywhere in the world –
where folk are starving?

What is that?
We asked, seeing it lying
white on the ground, like frost
in the first light.
'Take and eat,' said Moses.
And we did, and it was good.
But what is it?
'That is the bread
which the Lord has given you to eat.'
And we called it 'What is that?'
(manna)
And we gathered as much as we could eat,
enough to meet our needs.

Why not?
we asked, get more and save it for a hungry day?
But when we did
it rotted away.
And we, becoming wise, gathered
just enough bread.
For what?
To give us strength for the journey.

Where?
That's another question.

Jan Sutch Pickard

Elijah

(1 Kings 19:1–18)

I am Elijah
I fled for my life
a day's journey into the wilderness.
It could have been
a lifetime's journey,
for when I came to a broom bush
I sat down under its mocking bright flowers
and I prayed for death.
'It is enough,' I said,
'Lord, take away my life.
I have achieved nothing.
I am worth nothing.'
I lay down under the bush
hoping to die.
Instead, I slept.
Then an angel shook me awake
saying, 'Rise and eat.'
And there was a cake
baked on hot stones
and a pitcher of water.
Bed and breakfast in the wilderness!
I held the cake in my hand,
warm, crusty,
I bit into its grainy heart
and filled my mouth with its flavour.
I ate and drank
and lay down again.
Now would death come?
But the angel touched me again:

'Rise and eat:
the journey is too much for you.'
Again I ate the fresh bread
and it became
food for my journey.
Forty days and forty nights
I travelled on
towards the mountain of God –
encouraged by an angel,
sustained by bread.

Jan Sutch Pickard

The Birds
(Luke 12:16–26, Luke 9:11–17, Ex 16:13)

We are the birds
we neither sow nor reap.
We have no storehouse or barn,
but God feeds us.

There we were one day:
birds in the wilderness.
Down below, great crowds gathered –
that's not always good news for us.

Sometimes they expect us
to drop out of the sky to feed them!
And they're far too busy
wondering where their next meal
is coming from, to feed the birds.

But this time, something happened
down there on the ground
(we kept at a safe height).
Words were spoken, bread broken.
Suddenly there was enough
for everyone – and for us
crumbs – twelve basketfuls!

Life is more than food.
We take no anxious thought
for tomorrow,
we neither sow nor reap,
we have no storehouse or barn,
but God feeds us.

Jan Sutch Pickard

Jairus' Daughter

(Luke 8:40–42, 49–55)

I am Jairus' daughter.
Everyone called me 'child'.
Suddenly I was so tired.
Not hungry. It hurt.
I lay on my bed between sleeping and waking.
And I went a long way away
so I could barely hear my parents calling.

Then I heard the people crying,
wailing and crying
and I smelled the bread baking
to feed them all.
But I was only hungry
to be touched.
I was so lonely,
lying there and leaving home
and it got darker.

And then a hand took hold of mine,
a warm and friendly hand
and I heard someone saying
'Get up, my child.'
So I sat up, blinking
because it was bright daylight.
Why was I in bed?
Why was the house full of people?
Why was my mother crying?

The man holding my hand said
'Give her something to eat.'
And they brought me bread
warm from the oven.
Now I was hungry.
My hands were trembling.

He helped me to break it,
floury on my lips,
salty on my tongue,
filling my belly –
such good bread.
I ate every last crumb.
It tasted of life.

Jan Sutch Pickard

A Man
(Matthew 7:9)

I am a man
whose son asked him for bread
and who gave him a stone.

Only joking.
Boys don't cry.
Don't want him to become soft.
Got to learn to fend for himself,
fight his corner,
learn to be a breadwinner.

He held the stone in his small hand.
He looked me in the eye.
The tears were there,
but they didn't fall.
Things were never the same again.

There was no bread between us.

Jan Sutch Pickard

Canaanite Woman

(Matt 15:21–28)

I'm a Canaanite woman –
call me what you want,
I'm not going to argue this time.
I argued with Jesus
because my daughter was ill
and I knew he could heal her.
Don't ask me how I knew, I just did.
I shouted, 'Help me, Sir!'
and he said
'It's not right
to take the children's bread
and throw it to the dogs.'
Don't think I didn't care –
how would you like to be called a dog, a bitch,
as we are, daily, but I knew
that in his eyes
I was a human being. I just knew.
So I said

'Fair enough – but the dogs
get to eat the crumbs.'
And he smiled, and gave me
much more
than a crumb of comfort
under the table.
He gave my daughter health,
and he reminded me
that I am a human being, whole,
a child of God
who can sit with others round the table
and share the loaf.

Jan Sutch Pickard

A Family Man

(Luke 11:1–10)

I'm a family man –
We were all in bed
when the bloke next door
came asking for bread.

What a row he made
what a time to choose –
unexpected guests –
what a lame excuse.

Fed up, I yelled
'It's too late, you oaf:
We need our sleep!'
'But I need a loaf'

And he went on asking
and he went on knocking,
till – in spite of myself –
I was there, unlocking.

And now you tell me
that just the same
I should bother God
and not feel shame

To admit my need,
and ask to be fed –
with earthy prayers
for daily bread.

Jan Sutch Pickard

Cleopas

(Luke 24:13–35)

I'm Cleopas
  let me   catch my breath.
We've come back from Emmaus
without a moment's delay,
running most of the way
because Jesus   was there
at table with us
and we knew him when he broke the bread.
We'd walked   seven miles
with a stranger
barely noticing the road
under our feet.
Time passed
while we were deep in talk
about life, death,
broken dreams   rumour
a vision of angels
and, holding our breath,
the hope of the Messiah.

Afterwards we said
Weren't our hearts on fire as we talked?
That was why   reaching the door
we said
'Stay with us for the day is almost done.'

And then, at table
he took bread
said the blessing
and broke it to share –
and he was gone –
but look
we are here
to tell you all
to tell the world,
that we knew Jesus
    when he broke the bread.

Jan Sutch Pickard

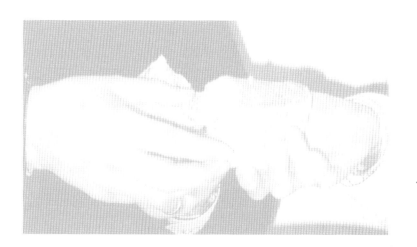

Wind is fresh on his face,
water laps at his feet,
a fire is ready
for the fish and bread meal
at the heart of his story.
Alone, he waits on the shore
for the fishers to come.

And they, with a catch
heavier than their dreams,
sail wondering into this story.
His greeting has the wholeness
of bread and poetry.
No word to suggest dogma or creed;
no ninety-nine impossible things
to believe before breakfast
but this one thing:
life … in all its abundance
… to be savoured and shared:
'Come and have breakfast'

Joy Mead

John 21:9–14

Kitchen Talk

Granary, Grant
and poppy-seed bloomer;
Cottage, coburg and cob;
    bread – warm from the womb
    of the oven – makes home
    a great smelling place;
    a place of belonging.

Danish, farmhouse,
Hovis and harvest sheaf,
spiral, twist and plait;
    bread – the delicious art of it,
    sculptural and shapely;
    the satisfying touch of it,
    pleasing to hands
    and eyes; wonderful
    to touch with teeth and tongue:
    fragile sharpness of crust,
    breaking into myriad pieces;
    moisty soft-white-crumb,
    chewy and voluptuous;
    or deep-rich-brown seediness,
    flavoured with autumn woods.

Bishop's bread and fougasses,
hot cross buns and challah;
    bread – waiting to become real
    in sharing and companionship;
    to nourish the body
    and feed the spirit.
Anadama Bread, Panis Lunatis,
Mexican bread of the dead;

bread: with its stories
to save for tomorrow.

Breadbaking, breadbreaking:
    best human activity
    creative, adventurous
    … and homely,
a way of being,
of walking lightly on the earth.
    Bread of belonging
    makes the homely place sacred,
    makes the sacred place earthy.
    Served in the kitchen;
    served at the altar:
    bread unites.
    Hunger for bread
    is hunger for humanness
    in us all.

Joy Mead

Most bread is more than itself and has a story

- **Anadama** is the one most bread books like to include. It's a traditional bread from Massachusetts, made with molasses, cornmeal, wholemeal and unbleached white flour. The legend tells that it was created by the husband of a woman called Anna. She'd left a cornmeal mush and some molasses in the kitchen. When he found only these ingredients for supper her husband mixed them with some flour, water and yeast to make this bread, muttering while he did so, 'Anna, damn her!' Perhaps not the most politically correct of stories – but at least he got on and made his own bread!

- **Maddybenny fadge** – a wonderful name! – the recipe comes from Rosemary White, of Maddybenny Farm, Northern Ireland. It's a potato bread – very good for breakfast.

- **Panis lunatis** means moon bread. In Switzerland, some believe it was the precursor to the croissant. Moon bread was baked as long ago as the 8th century.

- **Bread of the Dead** is made in Mexico around 2nd November, All Souls Day, and is an important part of celebration in memory of those who have died. This is not a time of sadness but a fiesta day. Families, wearing bright colourful clothes and carrying sweets and flowers, visit relatives' graves. They bring picnics which include this special bread, usually a white, yeast-risen dough, flavoured with orange and sometimes with spices. The bread – a simple round or a plaited loaf coiled into a circle – is decorated with pieces of dough formed into teardrops or bunches of flowers.

You'll find the recipes for these and the other breads in the poem in *The World Encyclopedia of Bread and Breadmaking* by Christine Ingram and Jennie Shapter or *The Bread Book* by Linda Collister and Anthony Blake. Details of these and other books appear on pages 154–155.

A Map of Bread

In Nazareth, Israel, warm, unleavened flat bread
eaten with hummus and olives
and local Palestinian dignitaries;
served with courteous formality,
the hospitality of the dispossessed,
and passionate subtexts.

In Phoenix, Mauritius, crusty baguettes
steaming from the oven of a Hindu baker
in a dusty Moslem town,
eaten with Chinese Christians,
a colonial legacy
to a multi-ethnic present.

In Sarajevo, Bosnia, pitta bread, kebab,
tiny cups of strong, sweet, cardamom-spiced coffee.
The crowded, cosmopolitan streets of this city
where Islam is at home,
a European faith,
buzz with conversation and culture heady in its richness.
But the still-shattered houses and charred hotels are silent witnesses
to a more brutal reality
and the potholed roads carry warnings
of landmines a few feet away.

In Moscow, Russia, solid, densely-textured white bread
with crunchy cucumbers.
The June trees green the city
and perestroika is in the air.
Women professors talk of fashion
of men who drink too much
of their children
of the rumour of possibilities.

In Naha City, Okinawa, not bread but rice,
pure white, unseasoned;
the Indians carry little pots of chilli to all the meals.
In the breakfast queue, the revolutionary leader in exile
speaks in measured tones of the slaughter of his people,
250,000 of them, invisible to western eyes.
Last year, fifteen years and many deaths later,
he finally went home.

In Harare, Zimbabwe, sticky sadza,
mealie porridge eaten with beautiful young women
who unaccountably die
between one meal and another.
Street children at the orphanage plant trees,
orange and lemon because 'there is no money for fruit'.
Harvest will not come in time for them.
They are planting for the future.

In Toronto, Canada, in a shop with eighty kinds of bread,
a man screams obscenities, threatens inexplicable violence
to the Korean shopkeeper.
She does not know him, nor any reason for his assault
but his hatred is palpable,
infects the other customers with fear.
Perhaps she did not have the bread
he was looking for.

'You shall eat, but not be satisfied,
and there shall be hunger in your inward parts.'
(Micah 6:14)

On the map of bread
so many hungers.

116

And we, the satiated,
the powerful
of state and church alike,
having bread,
decide who shall eat
and who shall go hungry.

Kathy Galloway

Eucharist is:

    breakfast by a lake,

    picnic by the sea,

    a dinner party,

    shared sandwiches,

    supper in a kitchen

    community lunch,

    tea together,

    food for a journey

    a meal on a mountain

    with thousands:

    bread and fish for all

    and baskets to fill

    with left-overs

Eucharist is:

    heaven in breaking bread and sharing;

    breaking open our understanding

    of a story … so a miracle

    is allowed to happen

    again.

Joy Mead

Eucharist ... and Children

For as long as I have thought adult thoughts, I have been disturbed by the custom of substituting a blessing for food when children come to the Table. I was pleased to see things begin to change and small children quite naturally accepting bread and wine when offered. This is surely how it is meant to be – children understand eating, children understand exclusion. Isn't the Eucharist a symbol of what is happening, or our vision of what is happening, within the world all the time – the great feast of life shared by all people? Bread and wine are gifts from our good earth and symbols of all food given to share with one another. As someone who has prepared and served food to family and friends for years I know that I would never offer the blessing of good food to the adults and the blessing of words and touch to the children! So what sort of symbol is the Eucharist service if that is what happens? There is surely holiness and wonder in all shared meals. That, I feel, is what Jesus meant when he suggested we remember him in the sharing of bread and wine. The story won't work if we are mesmerised by sign and symbol. We need a sense of the wonder of the ordinary. The Eucharist has power to transform but surely the transformation is not in a special set-aside place but in our ordinary everyday lives and at our ordinary everyday meals.

This goes further I fear. For if when we share food we bypass the most vulnerable members of our community, what does that say of us and what hope is there for those excluded from life's feast? My hope has always been that changing the symbolism of the Eucharist would change thinking – a transformation no less – so that rich and powerful would share with small and vulnerable on equal terms.

Joy Mead

Grace

(written by Daniel, Samantha and Greg
three children staying at The MacLeod Centre: 25.9.99 – 2.10.99)

Making bread –
squishy dough
moist feel
smelling of yeast,
punching, kneading
folding in air –
hard working hands.

White, brown, granary,
soft or crusty –
now we're baking!
Hot –
hungry smell.

Breaking, eating, sharing
Bread for everyone –
Communion!

Jam for Today?

There's a story told of a church that did not usually invite children to share the bread and wine at communion. After the service the minister was at the door to say his goodbyes. Bread and wine, remaining from the service, were on the Table still. As always, the Communion Steward cleared the Table and took the left-overs to the Vestry. Later the minister returned to the Vestry to find the steward and a group of enthusiastic children sharing the remaining bread, generously spread with jam. All were tucking into an unorthodox eucharist!

Joy Mead

Bread and Oars - God's Energy

In his book *Iona, God's Energy*, Norman Shanks, the Leader of the Iona Community, reflects on the way worship on Iona 'seeks to make the connections with everything else that is going on – by involving the people, by reflecting on the shared experiences – but in such a way as not entirely to exclude "outsiders".' He includes this reflection by Liz Gibson:

> *The bread for the Communion is made in the kitchens of the Abbey and MacLeod Centre. It can be a powerful experience for someone working as a volunteer cook to find that not only can they make meals but their work can create the central focus of worship. It brings the whole congregation closer to understanding the symbolism of the Eucharist.*
>
> *During the summer of 1997, as part of the Columba celebrations, a crew rowed from Ireland to Iona. On their arrival, just as the Sunday morning service was starting, they walked up the aisle each carrying an oar. The physical effort of rowing was itself an act of worship – by finishing in the Abbey rather than at the jetty they made a powerful statement and included the congregation in their experience. These examples, of bread and oars, are just two ways of symbolically showing how what we do outwith the church walls can enrich worship within.*

Eucharistic Nudgings

I have not tried to express what I am writing in this way before. It has to do with an increasing awareness that the mystery of the Eucharist is larger than eucharistic liturgies and eucharistic living – though both are more fundamental than I first thought. What I feel after has to do with what I will clumsily call the mass at the heart all creation. That is how things are. And our altars and liturgies provide glimpses and draw us into this pervading and transforming mystery.

What is emerging has taken place in the context of what I will call eucharistic deprivation. Physical circumstances over the last eight years have affected my relationship to and perception of the Church's eucharistic practice. For long periods I have been unable to be present inside church buildings to share in congregational Eucharists. The so-called deprivation has deepened the longing, encouraged the explorations and enabled the making of connections that I have not made before.

What of these eucharistic nudgings?
When we first arrived in our new neighbourhood we were warmly welcomed but told, 'We don't go into each other's houses.' Our neighbours are significant for both of us so on my short daily walks I made a point of hanging around to chat. All kinds of things can be shared at the end of a garden path! In time these conversations led to invitations to share coffee. Eventually we took the plunge and asked if people would like to bring food and drink to share a meal. We all talked in a way we have rarely done before. *And something for good happened in the sharing.*

There have been many other such shared meals. One was in a Balti Restaurant in Balsall Heath with sixteen people many of whom had only met briefly before and some of whom were struggling with language and culture. And during the meal four of the largest naan breads I have ever seen were broken as neighbour became aware of the needs of neighbour and we laughed … and were watched over by the large smiling Muslim proprietor. *And something for good happened in the sharing.*

An onlooker, through television, of another meal – aid workers driving large lorries full of bread into refugee camps during the Kosovo crisis and throwing bread into the outstretched hands of girls and boys, women and men – I wonder *what has to happen* to link again bread we break at the altar and bread we throw to the desperately hungry?

What of eucharistic living?
Michael Wilson had worked in Ghana as a doctor. On return he became a priest working on the staff of St Martin in the Fields and later in the Theology Department of Birmingham University. He was the nephew of Edward Wilson who went with Scott to the Antarctic where both of them died.

About eighteen months ago, when he was in his mid-eighties, Michael asked if I would be what he called his eucharistic person during the concluding period of his life. He lived with a huge cancerous tumour in his neck. I quickly learned that the invitation was much more than a prearranged devotional sacramental slot on a Thursday afternoon. Michael was much more interested in what he called eucharistic living than eucharistic liturgies. 'Eucharistic living,' Michael said, 'is about being open to receive the gifts of God through dark and light, through the creative and destructive, through the essential otherness of those who are different.' We explored what it could mean to lay ourselves open to receive the gifts of God through people of different world faith communities, different sexual orientation and different cultural backgrounds; to receive and to lay ourselves open to the possibility of transformation. In the Eucharist we say: God gives himself within the membranes of life and draws us into the mystery of providing within unexpected ways and places.

Eucharistic living is about experiencing and expressing gratitude. Michael would have warmed to old Cyril in Notting Hill who on receiving bread at the communion table murmured not a pious 'amen' but a shrill 'thank-you' for God's goodness in circumstances that most of us would find hard to bear.

Sometimes when I visited Michael there was the smell of freshly baked bread – made by his wife Jean. Often he greeted me from his chair with 'Come and see' and led me into the garden to look at a shrub, plant, flower or bush. He found immense joy and wonder in creation. Sometimes he missed church on a Sunday morning and went off with his sons to a bird sanctuary and returned both exhausted and exhilarated. He said once: 'When we arrive at the gates of heaven we will be asked one question: Have you found delight in my creation and delight in each other?' Over and over again he reminded us that it is God's intention that we find joy in each other.

Eucharistic living is also about sharing. 'The unshared remains unredeemed.' Some of us have grown impatient with the Church's eucharistic practice that individualises, privatises, spiritualises and institutionalises the bread-sharing of Jesus amongst the people. Michael explored radical alternatives that require no churchly priest. I wish that he had lived to hear of what is being explored and expressed through Barbara, Sheila and Linda in Liverpool. They make bread and share it, often with people who don't trust the Church institution enough to enter it and yet who are still prepared to explore the mystery of yeast, of kneading and rising, within their own stories and the stories of their communities. Companions, we are reminded, are those who share the bread of life.

I wonder what all this could mean, where it could lead, and I am left with a question that keeps on returning and won't go away: 'Who in the world are the priests and where are the altars?'

Donald Eadie

Tasting of Life – Bread in the City

We are Methodists in Liverpool city centre, without a church building or gathered congregation. I am, officially, the Superintendent of Liverpool City Centre Methodist Circuit, Linda is a probationer minister, Sheila is a member of a local church. Other members of the team include a teacher, an accountant and an inspector of taxes.

We are listening attentively to the city as we discover what God is doing already. Whilst we listen and wait we are having conversations with whoever will talk with us. We have particular contact with refugees and asylum seekers, office and shop workers, people on the street. And baking bread is our meeting point. Bread crosses boundaries in a post-sectarian city. It crosses thresholds with those who don't do church. It crosses barriers when stories lie deep and unheard. Our hope is to find new ways to become church as we find life in the fragile environment of the city

Barbara Glasson

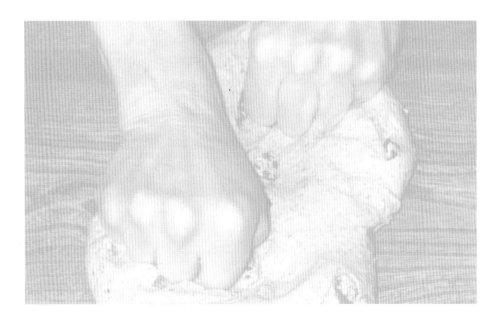

Iona

Not a spiritualised, far away
up in the clouds
eucharist
with de-valued wine in clinical glass
and orderly square
of cut, white bread;
but a rich, wholesome love feast
with a real brown loaf,
grainy and gutsy,
warm and sensual,
smelling of life,
broken and uneven,
trusting in its earthiness,
in its fleshiness:
a total union
of heaven and earth,
spiritual and physical
in joyful oneness
that heeds the questioning angel*
and no longer looks for glory
in the distance of the sky.

Joy Mead

*Acts 1:11

A Fragment of Bread

A fragment of bread
cupped in my hand
torn off from the whole
cupped in my hand
passed to me

And I too must tear the body
to share with my neighbour
a fragment of bread
to embody me with them
and he with us

A piece of bread
a bread of peace
scattered, grown
cut down, mown
gathered, ground
mixed and pummelled
risen, fired and found

A piece of bread
a bread of peace
sliced and toasted
broken, shared
around a table
to give us life.

Kate McIlhagga

The Last Supper

All day they are in the house:
Mary and Martha, Joanna and Salome,
Susannah and all the others,
baking bread,
making ready,
remembering together
other meals:
by the Sea,
on the mountain,
at Emmaus …
and always hoping
there will be enough
to go round.

They move quietly
in the space

between the lines
of his story,
making a ceremonial
of love out of everyday meals.
From the beginning
they have served and shared:
memories and hopes
dreams and visions,
common friendship.

He takes the unleavened bread,
the bread of parting and haste,
the bread of our sadnesses,
passes it from man to woman,
woman to man,
from man to child,
child to woman;
from hand to hand,
lips to lips –
that with light and leavened remembering
all may feast
on immortal grain.

Joy Mead

Mark 14:12–25

(This is a timeless poem about a timeless event – don't fall into the trap of trying to put the chronology right!)

Magnificat Now

(for Bob Holman)

The birthing of the ordinary
revolution: women's voices
sound Magnificat
making an enormous YES

on housing estates
and travellers' sites,
in hostels for the homeless
and cardboard cities;

in community food shops,
credit unions,
soup kitchens
and baby co-ops;

where the rhythm of a song
moves the people's dreams
like flowers scattered
at the site of a stabbing;

where the handmaid
of the Lord, in her own
shaft of light
stands tall and empowered
breaking each day
in community
the 25p sliced bread
of life.

Joy Mead

At Llyn y Fan Fach

Like a bowl of milk
the mountain cups the lake
where the Ages of Stone,
Bronze and Iron left their bones
under the earth, under the water
with the lake king's daughter.

*

Every day he dreamed her face
a ferment on the water surface
from the moment the sun first cast
its net of light from the east.
With his mother's bread
he'd win her to his bed.

The spell was buttermilk and barm,
grains ground between stones,
pummelled and set to warm
by a wood-fire or under the sun.
Such leavening as suddenly she'd break
the waters of the lake.

Three loaves,
three chances
to be lovers.
His offer. Her answer.
So he waded in from the land
till she took bread from his hand.

On the third day she was his own.
Three strikes of metal, she was gone.
The ages drown, dissolved into the past,
the stories of the lake lie lost
in archaeology, the myths and silts
of ancient settlements.

*

November.
The wind is bitter
and the air is stone.
We throw bread on the water
for a wild swan near the shore,
paddling alone.

Gillian Clarke

Christmas Eve: Notting Hill

Carrying this bread
through the midnight city,
I am a passer-by, stepping
over the broken glass,
uneven pavements, the dark puddles;
past houses curtained, shrugging off the street,
screenlit;
past hoardings with their obscenities
and philosophies;
sidestepping clinches and wrangles –
blows struck in a confusion of feelings;
past empty houses and empty faces;
under the motorway –
a progression of lights
from nowhere to nowhere,
an unreal and concrete heaven.

Carrying this bread,
newly baked, and midway
between conception and birth,
I bear a secret
older and more enduring
than the city: a fragrance
against the petrol fumes,
a growing thing, to rock these barren towers,
and heal the self-destruction of these streets.
I carry this bread
to be shared among
waiting people in the still church.

Carrying this bread,
I am caught up

in living patterns of the city.
Not a passer-by, but becoming part
in what I fear, and what links me to others.
The bread I bear now
and the child that I will bear
in the uncertain future –
my strength and my being,
our strength and our being.
Because of these, I am threatened.
Yet I walk safely
through the midnight streets,
carrying myself in two hands
and something more than myself –
the weight of a world.

Jan Sutch Pickard
(24.12.76)

First Communion

Fifty-four years on a hill I've been
waiting for the wind to blow
and all it did was blow the other way.

Sixty-six women and a few men and kids.
Two of them specially got up at five
so as to be ready with this and that.

This was a corn sheaf, tacky, maybe varnished,
and that was sage, which means something,
I don't know what. The incense wouldn't light.

Someone played a flute, I only noticed
when it stopped. Dancing also ended
so we were still, and maybe wondering

what they would do, the two of them
or we either. It was wonderfully simple,
they took a wooden bowl of seeds, a clay

goblet with sips of strong drink where you
could see an imprint of the potter's rough thumbs
and waited for the wind to blow the spirit round.

I knew, seventeen women and a few men and kids
away, that this would be for me, true.
Fifty-four years of waiting fell down the hill

and I stood wet, alone, and part of it all.
There was nothing that was not me,
or Spirit, or wonder, or seed, or dancing.

Alison Leonard
(15.12.98)

Bread for the Birds

My cup is running over:
I am pouring tawny wine
back into the earth,
from which it came
through the rising sap of the vine
and ripening grapes.

I am standing in the noon sun
on a green hill
in the living centre of creation;
under my feet the loom of grass
is woven with small flowers –
violet, primrose, celandine, speedwell;
above blueness billows like linen on a line.

I am scattering bread for the birds –
one loaf broken,
first shared among folk,
now crumbled on to the blue and green
picnic cloth of the day –
inviting white wings
which hover over my head.

I am in a state of amazed grace
on this day, unique and eternal –
wine poured out,
bread broken,
feet on the ground
and the sky full of wings.

Jan Sutch Pickard
(16.5.99)

Soul Bread

(for Ruth)

Travelling
through a black and white landscape
sustained by soul bread.

As far as the eye can see,
snow patterned plough-land,
vines and orchard trees
standing to attention in their sleep.

Grey waters under grey sky;
white birds taking wing.

Here in my hand,
as I gaze from the train window,
coarse bread
flecked with white salt crystals
and dark aniseed –
the staff of life,
soul food
unfamiliar and sustaining:
offered with love
for a journey far from home.

Jan Sutch Pickard
(November 1999)

Coming Down to Earth

In the breadshop,
among homely smells
and human conversations,
I started to weep with joy:
for the dailiness of bread
and shared meals,
people meeting and needs met,
the sacraments
of love and laughter.

Jan Sutch Pickard,
(after Iona, Easter 1993)

Martha

(John 11:11–43)

On the well travelled path
where earth stands firm
and stones slumber
mute, undisturbed, guarding
the essence of her story
she meets the one
who is always coming.

She has not taken the easy way
of passive acceptance.
She is angry:
'You are late; if you had been here
this would not have happened.'
Her misery will not destroy or drain

the energy of her crazy hope.
She brings to his coming
her own rich earthiness
absorbed from cooking bread
and feeding people
that they might live.

For he comes, her colourful Christ,
on tired, dirty feet
to a grey and ordinary place
where the smell of death
is all encompassing.
But where he knows,
amidst stink and stench,
the need to loosen
and let go,
to lighten and let free
the creative healing energy
of meeting and becoming
that out of deepest sorrow
will walk forth
life and hope.

Joy Mead

Let It Happen ...

(Matthew 14:13–21)

What did we expect?
How did we imagine
a meal would be made?
By logic? By reason?
By economics? By market forces?

No! Women and baskets!
The surprise of the ordinary!
Thousands fed by love!
An everyday miracle
we will not allow
to happen today.

***

Let it happen
this most ordinary of miracles:
sharing water, bread, fish cheese, fruit –
the contents of women's baskets
haven't changed very much.

Let it happen
the greatest miracle of all:
that people see
how things could be different,
see the hidden wisdom,
of the ones not counted

Let it happen:
sit down with those not counted;
stop organising,
stop doing good works.
Start trusting, risking, hoping
… and sharing.
Just open your baskets
and let people be.

Joy Mead

I, Like You

I, like you
cherish love, life, the sweet enchantment
of things, the blue landscape
of the days of January.

Also my blood pulsates,
I laugh with my eyes
that have known the outbreak of tears.
I believe that the world is beautiful,
that poetry is like bread, it belongs to everyone.

And that my veins don't end in me
but rather in the unanimous blood
of those who struggle for life,
love,
the things,
the landscape and bread
the poetry of all.

Roque Dalton

146

Cartmel

In the church there is a cupboard
and on the shelf a loaf of bread.
A common loaf, not without ambiguities.

But this is no holy of holies:
the cupboard has no doors,
is far back in the nave,
set at eye-level, within reach
of the poor of the parish,
hungry travellers (and maybe church mice).

A dusting of flour on the dark wood –
a blessing of good intention.

For centuries the bread –
a farsighted bequest, about local need –
has been renewed faithfully:
fragrance of fresh baking
like incense in the aisles.

Now the week-old bread
goes regularly to feed the ducks.

For today there are fewer pilgrims,
vagrants and travellers bypass the church.
The poor of the parish are less visible
and their hunger takes a different form

from the loaf, still offered
on an open shelf
in the empty church.

Jan Sutch Pickard
19.10.99

147

Be gentle
When you touch Bread
Let it not lie
Uncared for ... unwanted
So often
Bread is taken for granted
There is so much beauty
In Bread
Beauty of sun and soil
Beauty of patient toil
Winds and rain have caressed it
Christ so often blessed it
Be gentle when you touch Bread

Old Scottish verse

Pilgrim Bread

Touch tenderly: earth, water, air,
salt, time and broken grain –
this one life
in all. Touch
with loving hands;

hands to make
to shape and mould,
warm, moisty dough,
feeling fleshy,
smelling earthy;

hands to bake,
well crusted bread
set by the sun,
transformed by fire,
warm with wonder;

hands to break
and break again
pilgrim bread
for pilgrim people.

In the kitchens,
from the tables,
priests of the moment
we dare to serve
this quiet mystery
this risen life,
gift of the earth,
gift of our hands,
for all to share.

Joy Mead

A hymn for bread sharers:

Hands Shaped Like a Cradle

Put peace into each other's hands
and like a treasure hold it,
protect it like a candle-flame,
with tenderness enfold it.

Put peace into each other's hands
with loving expectation;
be gentle in your words and ways,
in touch with God's creation.

Put peace into each other's hands
like bread we break for sharing;
look people warmly in the eye:
our life is meant for caring.

As at communion, shape your hands
into a waiting cradle;
the gift of Christ receive, revere,
united round the table.

Put Christ into each other's hands,
he is love's deepest measure;
in love make peace, give peace a chance
and share it like a treasure.

Fred Kaan

It is Made of Bread …

a story by Nigel Collinson

The prison chapel was full of young men: impressive to see so many of them in church that grey Sunday morning, sad to reflect on the mixture of circumstance that brought them there. At the end of the service someone came forward and said, 'We would like to give you this.'

In his hand he held a small model of a woodland scene, about the size of a moderately sized paper-back. There was a log of wood on its side, alongside of which sprouted mushrooms and brightly painted toadstools. A blackbird perched on the log, butterflies too. And nearby a rather surprised mole popped out of its mole-hill, surrounded by ladybirds.

It was all beautifully modelled and beautifully painted. 'We would like you to have this to remember us by,' he said. 'I didn't do it. He did,' pointing to someone else sitting four rows back.

So I went up to *him* and he told me all about it. 'It is made of bread,' he said. 'We have five rounds a day and I do not eat them all. So I have made the model out of the bread I did not eat, baked it hard on the pipes running through my cell, stuck the pieces together, painted them … and it's for you.'

The model still sits on my bookshelves. The paint's now a little faded but on the side of the log is painted Psalm 23. I never did ask him why he chose Psalm 23; I guess the small woodland scene was the 'pastures green' through which we are led by the hand of God, a far cry from a prison cell, expressing something of longing perhaps, longing for something not seen. But for me it is a reminder of daily bread, not thrown away, but changed in strange circumstances by the hidden grace of God, the grace of God for which 'I shall not want'.

Bread Blessings

Blessing of sacred seed to you;
Blessing of waving wheat to you;
Blessing of golden harvests to you;
Blessing of sharing bread to you;
and all who eat with you.

Take, eat
bread of life
and love; take, eat
body of all things,
fruit of the earth:
a gift
for ordinary meetings,
at ordinary meals.

Joy Mead

Helpful and Interesting Books

Recipes and background material:

The Bread Book and *Country Bread*, both by Linda Collister and Anthony Blake (Conran Octopus) – I recommend these beautiful books with recipes, photographs and interesting bits and pieces about bread.
The Enchanted Broccoli Forest, Mollie Katzen (Ten Speed Press) – a charming book with a good section on breadmaking.
The Village Baker, Joe Ortiz (Ten Speed Press)
English Bread and Yeast Cookery, Elizabeth David (Penguin) – a classic with lots of recipes, quotes and general information.
Baba Á Louis Bakery Bread Book. The Secret Book of the Bread, John McLure (Baba Á Louis Bakery, USA, available in the UK from Green Books)
The World Encyclopedia of Bread and Breadmaking, Christine Ingram and Jennie Shapter (Lorenz Books) – a full-colour visual catalogue of the breads of the world: recipes and stories.

The Flour Advisory Bureau is another useful source of information. Several pictures from their publications have been used in this book. They will be happy to advise or supply pictures, recipes, etc. You might like to visit their website: www.fabflour.co.uk

Also, *Corn Milling* by Martin Watts (Shire Publications) has interesting information about watermills and windmills.

Poetry

Read some Gillian Clarke, especially *Letter From a Far Country,* published by Carcanet, 1982. Other books: *The King of Britain's Daughter, Selected Poems, Collected Poems* and *Five Fields* all published by Carcanet.
Talking to the Bones, Kathy Galloway (SPCK, 1996)
Selected Poems, David Scott (Bloodaxe Books, 1998)
The Greatest Gift, Angus Peter Campbell (Fountain Publishing, Isle of Skye, 1992)

And others …

Women's Prayer Services (Twenty-Third Publications,1987)

Inside Stories, Angela Wood and Robin Richardson (Trentham Books, Westview House, 734 London Road. Oakhill, Stoke on Trent, Staffs, ST4 5NP) – a delightful book of and about stories.

Piece Together Praise, Brian Wren and *The Only Earth We Know*, Fred Kaan (Stainer and Bell) – both with lots of good 'bread' hymns.

Courses

Andrew Whitley (see pages 71–77) runs breadmaking courses – **Bread Matters** – in his beautiful bakery in Melmerby

Spend a stress-free weekend in the North Pennine village of Melmerby and go home with a basketful of your own bread, fresh from the brick oven. Absolute beginner, occasional exponent or regular devotee – whatever your starting point, I guarantee two days of hands-on enjoyment as I reveal the secrets of the artisan bread and yeasted pastries which I have been making for over 20 years …

I will guide you through the fundamentals of fermentation on which all good bread depends. Alone, or in small groups, with help from myself and a fellow baker, you can embark on a baking journey from sourdough rye to flavoured flatbread, from poppy seed rolls to pain de campagne.

And as we share experiences, relaxing over meals in the award-winning Village Bakery Restaurant, I will enjoy telling you how the bakery began when I left London equipped with little more than a burning conviction that bread matters.

Andrew Whitley

Want to know more? Contact Andrew Whitley at The Village Bakery, Melmerby, Penrith, Cumbria CA10 1HE. Tel: 01768 881515, fax: 01768 881848, email: Andrew@village-bakery.com; website: www.village-bakery.com

Notes

Cover picture: Tim Hazael

The World Council of Churches commissioned a small design and production company, IKON, to produce a study pack on the theme *Choose Life*. They wanted to include a picture of breaking bread. IKON's office was in central London, near Neal's Yard bakery, so Tim Hazael went round the corner and bought a fresh crusty loaf. Looking for hands to break it, he co-opted a body-builder from a gym in the same building. He, with great zest, broke the bread and Tim Hazael took the photograph. I'm grateful to Jan Sutch Pickard for the background story and to Tim Hazael and the World Council of Churches for permission to use the photograph.

Part One

Pages 19/20: 'Because of the Seed', from *Inside Stories*, Robin Richardson and Angela Wood (Trentham Books Ltd, Westview House, 734 London Road, Oakhill, Stoke-on-Trent, Staffs ST4 5NP, 1992, p.10).

Page 26: 'Seed is Sacred' from the One World Week Study Guide, 1995: *Growing Hope* (p.24).

Page 26: 'Bere' by Peter Leith and One World Week participants on Orkney, from One World Week Study Guide 1995: *Growing Hope* (p.27).

Page 27: 'Seedlings' by Dhyanchand Carr, India, from *Dare to Dream*, ed. Geoffrey Duncan (Fount, 1995, p.214) © Christian Conference of Asia: from 'Patterns of Witness in the Midst of Religious Plurality', CCA News July/August 1993.

Page 34: Illustration: Barnsley Metropolitan Borough Council.

Page 39: 'Refugee' was first published in *Wisdom is Calling* (Canterbury Press, 1999)

Page 41: George Mackay Brown tells this story in 'The Midsummer Music' in *An Orkney Tapestry* (Victor Gollancz Ltd, 1969).

Page 42: 'Song of Africa' included in *Discovering God's Abundance* (The Methodist Church, 1992, p.37), source unknown.

Page 43: 'Song of Communion', *The Nicaraguan Campesino Mass*, Carlos Jejia Godoy and Pablo Martinez, Nicaragua, taken from *Women's Prayer Services*

(Twenty-Third Publications, Connecticut, 1987).

Page 44: 'A Hymn on Not Giving Up' from *The Only Earth We Know*, Fred Kaan (1989 Hope Publishing Company for USA and Canada, Stainer & Bell for all other territories).

Page 46: Photo by courtesy of the Orkney Library – Photographic Archive.

Part Two

Page 61: Illustration: Breadmaking at the MacLeod Centre, Iona, Jan Sutch Pickard

Page 66: 'The Spirit of Bread' extract reprinted with permission from *The Village Baker: Classic Regional Breads from Europe and America* (p.2) , © 1993 by Joe Ortiz (Ten Speed Press, USA). Available online at www.tenspeed.com

Page 67: 'Leaven' is based on information from the *Baba Á Louis Bakery Bread Book*, John McLure (Baba Á Louis Bakery, USA, 1993). See suggested reading on page 89.

Page 68: Illustration: Breadmaking in Burkina Faso from *Lifelines*, published by Christian Aid; photographer: Karin Nyffenegger.

Page 79: This poem is based on a story which appeared in *The Guardian* during 1998 and the quote from Pelagius is taken from 'The Four Letters of Pelagius' which appear in *Celtic Spirituality,* ed. Oliver Davies (Paulist Press).

Page 82: Illustration: Maria Doras making tortillas for a family in Quibute, Nicaragua: Christian Aid/David Pearson.

Page 83: '… Maker of Heaven and Earth …' by Kathy Galloway from *Talking to the Bones* (SPCK, p.55).

Page 84: The prayer comes from a Christian Aid card with the picture on page 82.

Page 85: 'Communion Calypso' from *The Only Earth We Know*, Fred Kaan (1989 Hope Publishing Company for USA and Canada, Stainer & Bell for all other territories).

Page 86: Illustration from *Baba Á Louis Bakery Bread Book*, John MacLure.

Part Three

Pages 90–91: 'A Long Way from Bread' by David Scott from *Selected Poems* (Bloodaxe Books, 1998, pp.22–23).

Pages 92–94: 'Manna, Meaning What Is It?' by Angus Peter Campbell, from *The Greatest Gift* (Fountain Publishing, 1992, pp123–125).

Page 122: 'Bread and Oars' – an extract by Liz Gibson taken from *Iona, God's Energy*, Norman Shanks (Hodder and Stoughton, 1999, p.132).

Page 127: 'Iona' first appeared in *The Epworth Review*, May 1993.

Page 131: 'Magnificat Now' first appeared in *Coracle*, December 1999.

Page 132–133: Gillian says: *The Llyn-y-Fan Fach legend is extraordinary because it is the story of the ancestors of the famous family of the Physicians of Myddfai, renowned doctors, healers and herbalists, some of whom are buried in the church-yard at Myddfai in Carmarthenshire. A wonderful example of how myth is actually oral history, as understood by those who first put it into words. Another layer of meaning is given to us by the archaeologists, who tell us that the legend originates when the Stone Age people first encountered the Iron Age people, invading Celts wearing metal jewellery and bearing arms. Thus iron is a symbol of threat. It is an example of archaeological evidence arising from spoken language. As I see it, the lake is the past, into which successive 'ages' go, as the girl did.*

Page 140: 'Coming Down to Earth' by Jan Sutch Pickard, from *Celebrating Women*, ed. Janet Morley, Hannah Ward and Jennifer Wild (SPCK, 1995, p.94).

Page 141–142: 'Martha' first appeared in *The Epworth Review*, January 1996.

Page 143: 'Let it happen' first appeared under the title 'Women and Baskets' in *Connect*, Autumn 1998.

Page 145: 'I, Like You,' by Roque Dalton. Poem printed in a greetings card published by the Nicaragua Solidarity Campaign and reproduced with their permission.

Page 146: Illustration: Photo taken at Cartmel Priory.

Page 149: 'Pilgrim Bread' first appeared in *Connect*, Autumn 1997.

Page 150: 'Hands Shaped Like a Cradle' from *The Only Earth We Know*, Fred Kaan (1989, Hope Publishing Company for USA and Canada, Stainer & Bell for all other territories).

Photographs

I am grateful to:

Ian Mead for pages 53, 57, 78 and 126;

Elizabeth MacKenzie for pages 12, 16, 20, 22, 24, 25, 28, 41, 43, 45, 100, 107, 121, 129, 132, 133, 136, 140, 144, 152;

The Flour Advisory Bureau, 21 Arlington Street, London SW1A 1RN for pages 38, 40, 98, 101, 104, 111, 112, 114, 117, 121, 131.

Photographs on pages 31, 33, 35, 37, 73, 103, 105, 109, 118, 134, 141, 148, 153 are my own.

Thank you also to Anna and Tom Robinson (picture p.121) for eating bread and jam so enthusiastically and helpfully.

The Iona Community

The Iona Community, founded in 1938 by the Revd George MacLeod, then a parish minister in Glasgow, is an ecumenical Christian community committed to seeking new ways of living the Gospel in today's world. Initially working to restore part of the medieval abbey on Iona, the Community today remains committed to 'rebuilding the common life' through working for social and political change, striving for the renewal of the church with an ecumenical emphasis, and exploring new, more inclusive approaches to worship, all based on an integrated understanding of spirituality.

The Community now has over 240 Members, about 1500 Associate Members and around 1500 Friends. The Members – women and men from many denominations and backgrounds (lay and ordained), living throughout Britain with a few overseas – are committed to a fivefold Rule of devotional discipline, sharing and accounting for use of time and money, regular meeting, and action for justice and peace.

At the Community's three residential centres – the Abbey and the MacLeod Centre on Iona, and Camas Adventure Camp on the Ross of Mull – guests are welcomed from March to October and over Christmas. Hospitality is provided for over 110 people, along with a unique opportunity, usually through week-long programmes, to extend horizons and forge relationships through sharing an experience of the common life in worship, work, discussion and relaxation. The Community's shop on Iona, just outside the Abbey grounds, carries an attractive range of books and craft goods.

The Community's administrative headquarters are in Glasgow, which also serves as a base for its work with young people, the Wild Goose Resource Group working in the field of worship, a bi-monthly magazine, *Coracle*, and a publishing house, Wild Goose Publications. Between Glasgow and Iona the Community now has a staff of almost 50 people and an annual turnover of around £1.4M.

For information on the Iona Community contact: The Iona Community, Pearce Institute, 840 Govan Road, Glasgow G51 3UU. Phone: 0141 445 4561
e-mail: ionacomm@gla.iona.org.uk   web: www.iona.org.uk

For enquiries about visiting Iona, please contact: Iona Abbey, Isle of Iona, Argyll PA76 6SN
Phone: 01681 700404   e-mail: ionacomm@iona.org.uk

For book/tape/CD catalogues, contact Wild Goose Publications, Unit 16, Six Harmony row, Glasgow G51 3BA   e-mail: admin@wgp.iona.org.uk
or see our products online at www.ionabooks.com